11 Easily Pieced Projects

Sensational Quilts

FOR SCRAP LOVERS

Color & Cutting Strategies

Judy Gauthier

C&T PUBLISHING

Text copyright © 2020 by Judy Gauthier

Photography and artwork copyright © 2020 by C&T Publishing, Inc.

Publisher: Amy Barrett-Daffin

Creative Director: Gailen Runge

Acquisitions Editor: Roxane Cerda

Managing Editor: Liz Aneloski

Editor: Kathryn Patterson

Technical Editor: Debbie Rodgers

Cover/Book Designer: April Mostek

Production Coordinator: Zinnia Heinzmann

Production Editor: Alice Mace Nakanishi

Illustrator: Kirstie L. Pettersen

Photo Assistant: Gregory Ligman

Photography by Estefany Gonzalez of C&T Publishing, Inc.,
unless otherwise noted

Published by C&T Publishing, Inc., P.O. Box 1456, Lafayette, CA 94549

Library of Congress Cataloging-in-Publication Data

Names: Gauthier, Judy, 1962- author.

Title: Sensational quilts for scrap lovers : 11 easily pieced projects :
color & cutting strategies / Judy Gauthier.

Description: Lafayette : C&T Publishing, [2020]

Identifiers: LCCN 2019051013 | ISBN 9781617458682 (trade paperback) |
ISBN 9781617458699 (ebook)

Subjects: LCSH: Patchwork--Patterns. | Quilting--Patterns.

Classification: LCC TT835 .G331795 2020 | DDC 746.46/041--dc23

LC record available at https://lccn.loc.gov/2019051013

Printed in the USA

10 9 8 7 6 5 4 3 2 1

Acknowledgments

I would like to thank the employees in my shop—Barb Bending, Laura Olson, Cindy Cody, and Kim Bates. It's because of your outstanding help and customer service that I was able to finish this book and all my other books before it. Because you have taken the projects home and finished bindings and run the shop like a well-oiled machine, I am able to produce these books.

I would also like to thank my husband, whose frequent dinners alone have enabled me to travel to promote my books.

Contents

Frontal Boundaries
28

True North
36

Argyle Sweater
42

Split Screens
50

Precious Metals
56

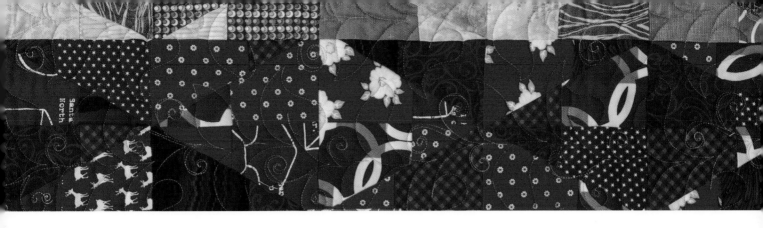

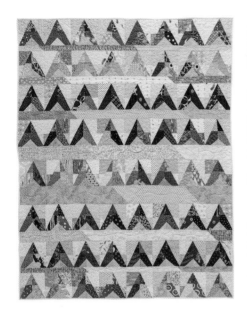

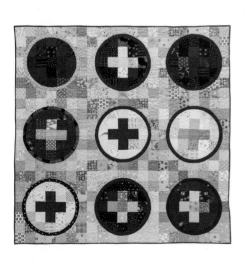

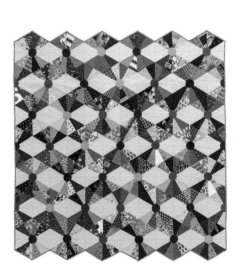

Introduction

Playing with my fabric scraps is my all-time favorite sport. After writing two other books about scrap quilting, *Quilts for Scrap Lovers* and *Rainbow Quilts for Scrap Lovers* (both from C&T Publishing, page 95), I am no less enthusiastic about it. My scraps mostly consist of leftovers from shop sample projects and garment sewing, and those pesky little ends of bolts that amount to about 4″ to 8″ at best. Most of these leave slightly larger scraps. They overwhelm me. My husband once asked me if anyone has ever climbed to the top of them and placed a flag there. It's a superhuman feat, to be sure.

All my scrap quilts are made using three sizes of templates: 3½″, 4½″, and 5½″ squares. These can be purchased commercially (such as fast2cut Simple Square Templates by C&T Publishing; see photo on next page) or made using your own method of producing a template. I highly recommend using a template for cutting those perplexing, oddly shaped scraps, which I'll explain further in the next section.

It also takes a little more time to "marry" scraps that are from widely diverse fabric populations. For instance, someone may have scraps from a baby quilt using juvenile fabric and scraps of fabric left over from making a shirt. Marrying these scraps together presents a particular challenge for quilters. People often wonder if it is indeed possible. Let me assure you, it is. It just takes a little finesse and some basic understanding of color.

If you can arrange scraps in a way in which the eye "expects" to see colors in a grouping or progression, you can hide and also enhance many fabrics from varied genres.

This book is designed not only to provide you with patterns for beautiful quilts but also guidance for fabric selection in your own works. This information is based on a combination of a great many years of experience and on the science of the color wheel, which never grows old.

Sit back and take in as much as you can.

What's So Special About These Sizes?

In my previous books about scrap quilting, my scrap quilts were all made using 3½", 4½", and 5½" squares. This work continues.

These wonderful little templates will assist you in making the quilts in this book. Because so many of my scraps are oddly shaped, they don't lend themselves to strip piecing. I often wonder about all those scrap quilt patterns that talk about taking a strip that is the "width of fabric" by a certain measurement. To me, those aren't scraps. I mean, sometimes I have scraps that are perfect like that but not often, unless I am using up what is left from the end of a bolt. Most of the time, they're left over from cutting out curves or garments, or fussy cutting something. So you don't get perfectly straight scraps. Do you make oven mitts? Bibs for babies? Garments? Do you cut curves for curved piecing? How about all those quilters that have die-cutting machines?

You need a system that works like a cookie cutter. That's why I love acrylic templates. You can just plunk these little gems down and cut around them with a rotary cutter, thereby allowing you to use up the largest part of the scrap or the smallest part of the scrap, wherever the template fits.

The next reason why these sizes are so wonderful is this—they have a least common multiple of 60, and 60 is a nice number for quilters. The least common multiple for 3 and 4 is 12. If you want to make a block using the 3½" template, you can make it a 12½" block by using a 4 × 4 layout of the 3½" templates. If you want to put a block next to that to make if fit, and you want to use the 4½" template, you know that you can make it 12½" as well, in a 3 × 3 layout.

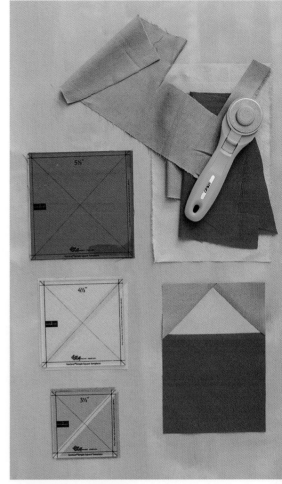

My fast2cut Simple Square Templates (page 95) make quick work of trimming your scraps.

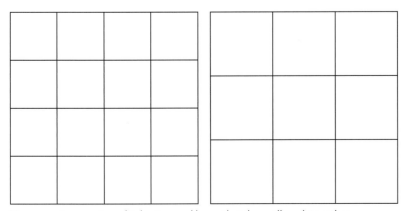

You can cut scraps in multiple sizes and know that they will work together.

This is the same for the 4½" template and the 5½" template. They have a least common multiple of 20. If you want to make up blocks using all 3 templates, the least common multiple is 60. There are many other common multiples as well. I have always encouraged my students in classes to use these to design their own blocks.

These sizes also combine well when cut into half- and quarter-square triangles. Here is a great example from my first book, *Quilts for Scrap Lovers*. It's one of the blocks from my quilt *Sunshine and Shadows*.

It's easy to come up with a lot of different blocks using these templates. It's a great way to use up your scraps when you have no clear direction for what you are going to do with them. If you limit yourself to these sizes, you are setting boundaries in your brain, and that helps you to narrow your focus. This is exactly what you need when you are paralyzed with thousands of possibilities.

This Sunshine and Shadows block uses all three sizes of templates for construction.

Using Odd Shapes and Bias Edges

I have given lectures on using my templates dozens of times, and each time I do, someone asks me if I worry about bias edges. My usual answer is no, because over the years I have learned how to handle them to prevent them from stretching. The newer sewists should avoid cutting their squares with bias on the outside edge or they will need to learn to treat the bias edges with respect.

I like to refer to the cut piece as a piecrust. (I'm sensing a common theme here … cookie cutters, piecrusts.) When you pick up a piecrust after rolling it out, and you put it into the pie plate, you will handle it very, very delicately. Your fabric square won't break apart, but it needs to be handled delicately. Avoid overhandling it. When you iron it, don't use the iron like a rolling pin. If you still have doubts and concerns, then cut a piece of interfacing and iron it to the back of the scrap. After you do this, cut the scrap using the template. This is the very best way to use every scrap without having to worry about having a bias edge.

Some people advocate for using spray starch to prevent bias edges from stretching. While spray starch does make fabric easier to handle and stiffens it, interfacing the piece is the best way forward if you truly want to prevent stretching on a bias edge. Not every scrap that you cut on the bias will need to be interfaced. That would be too time consuming. However, there are some fabrics that when cut on the bias are going to give you trouble. With time and experience, you learn to identify those.

The Keystone Block

There is one block that I use repeatedly. It is the same basic block, but each time I use it, there is a variation.

This block is addicting. Once you make it, you will find yourself going back to it over and over again. You will probably create your own variations. This block is beautiful on its own, and it looks dramatically different in a horizontal layout than it does with an on-point layout.

It's simple and fun to make because there's a stacking and cutting component to it. I have used it repeatedly in all my books because it is the perfect jumping-off point for many designs. Here's how it works.

Keystone block from *Treasure Box*
(full quilt, page 14)

Making the Keystone Block

1. Choose 2 high-contrast fabrics, such as a light and dark print or solid.

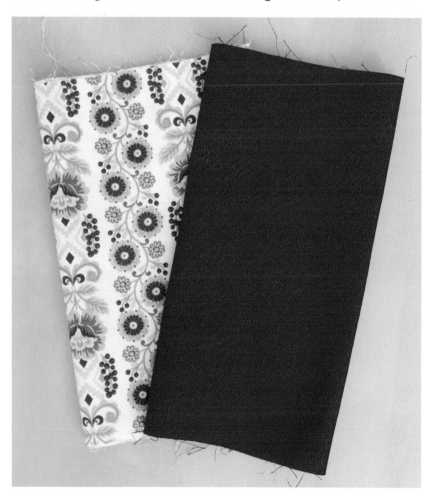

2. Cut 2 light squares and 2 dark squares using the 5½" square template, and align them in a stack.

Stack all 4 together.

3. Lay the 3½" template over the lower right corner, aligning the edges.

4. Snug the 5½" template up to the 3½" template.

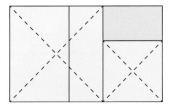

5. Hold the 5½" template in place while you remove the 3½" template and place it to the side of your work.

6. Using a rotary cutter and very sharp blade, cut along the edge of the 5½" template.

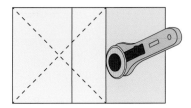

7. Move the narrow rectangles aside and replace the 3½" template at the bottom of the 3½" rectangle, aligning the edges.

8. Cut across the top of the 3½" template.

All cutting for this block is done!

9. Chain piece the rectangles to the squares, pairing the dark rectangles with the light squares and the light rectangles with the dark squares.

10. Press the seam allowances toward the dark fabrics. Stitch the long rectangles to the sides of the square/rectangle units. Press the seam allowances toward the rectangles.

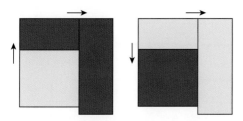

11. Trim the units so the ends of the rectangles are even with the squares.

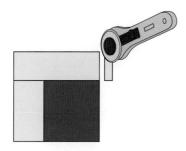

Some quilts that use this block require the entire block to be squared to 4½" × 4½". It can be squared using the 4½" template. The look of the block will change depending on where you lay the template. The block can be squared with the template over the rectangles so more of the square is trimmed off.

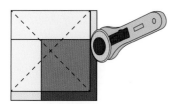

The block can also be squared with the template over the square so that more of the rectangles are trimmed off.

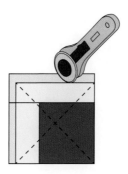

12. Sew the 4 units together like a four-patch.

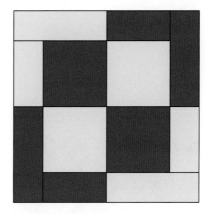

Here are a few fabulous examples of some of my quilts using this block. You will find even more quilts using this block throughout this book.

Treasure Box, 45³/₄″ × 45³/₄″

Complete instructions can be found in *Quilts for Scrap Lovers* (by Judy Gauthier, from C&T Publishing, page 95).

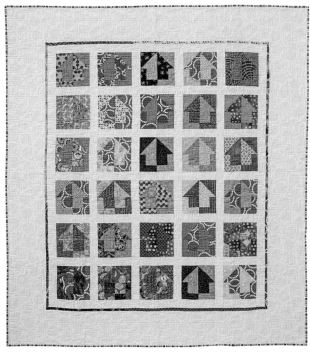

House Divided, 72¹/₂″ × 82¹/₂″

Complete instructions can be found in *Quilts for Scrap Lovers* (by Judy Gauthier, from C&T Publishing, page 95).

Packages, Boxes, and Bows, 80¹/₂″ × 80¹/₂″

Complete instructions can be found in *Rainbow Quilts for Scrap Lovers* (by Judy Gauthier, from C&T Publishing, page 95).

Systems of Color Selection for Scrap Quilts

Color selection is daunting. It's scary. When you're faced with a million scraps it's even worse.

Here's a course of action. Sort your scraps by color, but also by size. Look at the decision tree diagram below and follow along.

Scrap Organization Tree

Scrap color

Red, orange, yellow, green, blue, purple, pink, brown black, white/cream, gray

Scrap bin

Shelf
Anything greater than ½ yard

Fat quarter container

Do not split hairs during this initial sort. Don't agonize or worry whether something is blue/green or green/blue. Not yet. There will be time for that later. Sort your scraps according to color using the following colors: red, orange, yellow, green, blue, purple, pink, brown, black, white/cream, gray, and finally black-and-white. Prints that are almost exclusively black also go in the black-and-white bin.

I have a bin for "modern backgrounds." Anything that is white or cream that would make a good background print or background solid goes into this bin. Tan goes in this box as well, unless it is leaning way toward brown.

Fabrics that are black-and-white prints are a category unto themselves. I rarely use them in scrap quilting because I rarely use them, period. That's not because it's wrong but because I don't care to make black-and-white quilts. I have very few of these. Someone else may have a lot of them, and that's okay. When I use them, it tends to be white with black print, and it's usually used as a background.

Black-and-white prints used as a background in my quilt *Aromatic Rings*

If you're confused about what color a scrap really is, then ask a friend. But tell the friend that you need to decide which of the colors it is from the groupings (page 15). Pare it down to one of those colors and put it in the correct bin.

So, What Qualifies a Scrap to Be a Scrap?

I should probably clarify what I consider to be a scrap. In the scrap organization tree (page 15), I talk about size. Anything smaller than a fat quarter to me is a scrap. If it's large and it's left over from making a garment and it's not a fat quarter, then it's a scrap. For example, if I cut out a pair of pajamas, and I have a long, somewhat-wide piece of fabric that is fairly large but odd-shaped, then it's a scrap. If I have an intact fat quarter, then it's a fat quarter and not a scrap. These go into see-through wire drawers. If it's larger than a fat quarter and hasn't been cut into, then it's going to go on a shelf with fabrics of the same color.

My scraps are always at least 3½" × 3½" or else I give them away. I don't typically do scrap quilts with tiny, tiny pieces. There are many authors and people that do who don't find them to be too small.

If your pieces are tiny, all these guidelines are still applicable.

Color Theory

We've all been beaten to death with a stick about color theory. It still necessitates discussion.

I love to use a color wheel, and the one that I use the most is the Essential Color Wheel Companion (by Joen Wolfrom, from C&T Publishing).

The color wheel is based in science, and it never fails us. Here is a decision tree that I use when trying to decide what colors to use in a quilt.

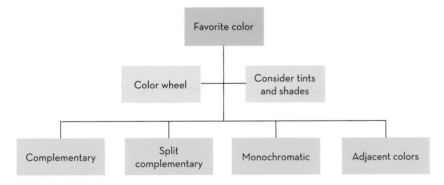

Remember, you should always be enjoying the process. We all know what it is like to have to make a quilt for someone else, when we may not like the colors that someone else chooses. Unless you're a quilter who makes his or her living by sewing for others, I would keep these unsatisfying experiences to a minimum.

I always tell customers in my shop to choose the fabric that makes their heart sing, and I mean it. Use that fabric that you fall in love with and absolutely makes you swoon, and then choose everything else around it.

Go to your scrap bin and find that piece. Use your favorite fabric or color. Then go to your color wheel and decide if you want to make a quilt with an analogous (adjacent) color scheme, a monochromatic color scheme, a complementary color scheme, or a split-complementary color scheme.

There's one other scheme that I have included under split-complementary and that is a *triadic color scheme*. If you draw an equilateral triangle on the color wheel, you will have all three points touching three different colors. If you turn the triangle multiple ways, it will touch three different colors each time. These three colors will always go well together in a quilt. I have lumped this under split-complementary because the colors really are complementary, and there are more than two.

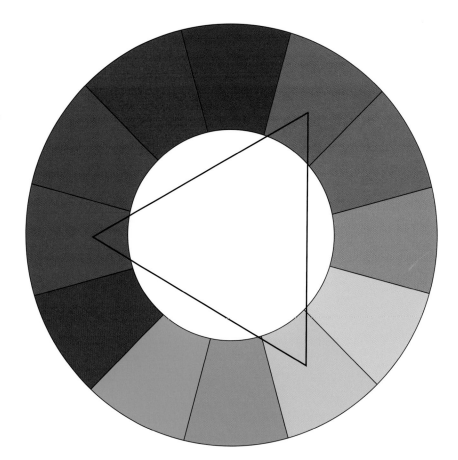

A **MONOCHROMATIC COLOR SCHEME** is just as it sounds—using all the same color in a quilt. I love to use this color scheme because sometimes you just have way more of one color in your stash of scraps than you do any other color. It's a great way to pull one bin and just go for it. Make a quilt using all one color. It's easy, it's uncomplicated, and it's fun.

A **COMPLEMENTARY COLOR SCHEME** is when you use a color and its exact opposite. It is always a good idea. It's appealing to the eye and what could be easier than two colors?

A **SPLIT-COMPLEMENTARY COLOR SCHEME** is when a color is used along with its adjacent colors, and then the color that is exactly opposite of it is used as a bit of a surprise. It's always beautiful.

Color Transitioning and Hiding Bizarre Prints

Now that you know the basic color combination schemes, it's much easier to grab up those bins full of colored scraps and just go to town. But I am going to throw a wrench in your works. Here it is.

Select your blue bin and start separating. Find the blue on the color wheel. Find a plain, true blue fabric and match it to the blue on the color wheel.

Dump your fabric from your blue bucket. Find a blue that is almost purple. Put it to the right of your plain blue.

Find a blue that looks like a greener blue and put it over to the far left of your main true blue fabric.

You have just established your blue color line. Fill in the spaces between the blue-purple and the blue-green. Find the blues that lean more green and the blues that lean more purple. Pay no mind to what the print looks like in the fabric, only the predominant color. Continue to pile like colors with like colors. This fun exercise not only will help you to familiarize yourself with subtleties in color but make you much more aware of all the colors in a color family.

Don't forget about tints and shades. Remember, navy blue is a shade of blue. Tints and shades can be used to introduce lights and darks in a block or quilt that is monochromatic.

After you have done this, take some of the scraps that are grouped closest to each other and make a quilt block using just those colors. In doing this you will see that the prints that are in the various pieces really take second stage to the actual color. You will notice that you can disguise a lot of "difficult to marry" scraps. When the colors are within the same color family and are of the same exact hue in the spectrum, the human eye is going to see the color in advance of picking up the print, even with large-scale prints. This is an optimal way to disguise odd prints.

Transitioning Colors That Are Not Color Wheel Neighbors

There are times when you want to move from one color to another and have a smooth transition. This can be difficult. This move can force you to use some fabrics from your stash that are not scraps in order to make that transition. You can also visit your quilting BFF or members of your guild and have a swap.

Let's say for example that you want to make a scrap quilt and your favorite color combination is red, yellow-gold, and mint green. I love this combination. In fact, there is a quilt in this book with this very combination, and a table runner in one of my other books with this combination!

Detail of *True North* (full quilt, page 36)

Cross My Heart, 16½" × 46½"

Complete instructions can be found in *Tantalizing Table Toppers* (by Judy Gauthier, from C&T Publishing, page 95).

You don't have to do a gradual transition, but the challenge is really fun. In *True North*, I have transitioned from red to pink, then to gold, and then to mint. The transition from red to pink is an easy one. Choosing red fabrics for the center, I gradually moved outward and chose reds that lean pink and pinks that lean red. Most quilt blocks in any quilt are pieced. There are many pieces in a block with which to make that transition. Transition occurs not only from block to block but from piece to piece within that block.

Detail of *True North* (full quilt, page 36). The pieces in the block feature fabrics that have two colors in them to allow for a transition to occur. Here I am transitioning from pink to the gold blocks.

Looking at the *True North* block (at left), it is easy to see that you need to find fabrics that contain both colors—the starting color, and the color that you are transitioning toward. Moving from red to pink is an easy transition, because pink is simply a tint of red. Moving from pink to gold is not as easy. There have to be fabric selections in which the print contains both pink and gold, or pink and yellow. This is where you start hunting for those fabrics either in your stash, your favorite shops, or from your quilting besties!

It will be amazing and surprising to you just how many fabrics will fit the bill. Pieces that you would never have expected to use will jump out at you. Once you find those pieces place them in the blocks. You will need to find multiple pieces with those color combinations. Gradually move from those into the next color. You can see from the photo (at left) that I have moved from the pink to the pink-and-gold prints into the gold. Stay in the gold colorway for the next outer ring or section of your quilt. The next step is to move from gold into the mint colorway. Again, you will be hunting for fabrics that combine gold and mint. Follow the same procedure to move into the mint colorway.

This is fun and exciting. Part of the thrill of making a quilt is the pursuit of the fabric. This will send you down a road of pursuit that will intensify your color experience.

Let's Talk About Piecing Curves

One quilt project in this book, *Circle Gets the Square* (page 80), uses curves. There are actually circles that are sewn into squares. This may seem daunting. A little practice goes a long way.

Several tools on the market make it easy to cut circles. While I don't endorse using a particular tool, I would like to explain various methods of cutting circles.

Measuring for Curves

There is a basic rule of thumb for cutting circles that will be sewn inside background circles with a ¼" seam. The background circle is always cut 1" smaller than the circle that goes inside. If you are setting a 9" circle into a background, the circle that is cut out of the background will be 8".

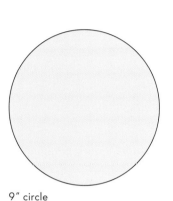

9" circle

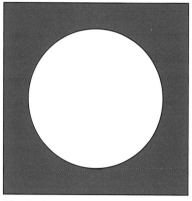

8" cutout

For *Circle Gets the Square*, the set-in circles are concentric rings. A 17" circle is placed into a circle cut from the background square. The background square is made up of smaller squares. This does not change the measurements. The circle cut from the background will be 16".

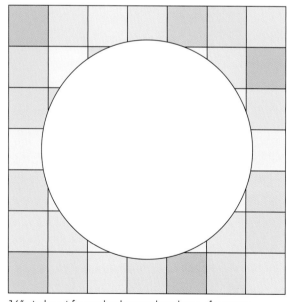

16" circle cut from a background made up of squares

It is helpful to press a very lightweight iron-on interfacing over the wrong side of the background before cutting out the circle. This helps to keep the bias edges from stretching.

Cutting the Curves

Specialized rulers for cutting circles work great. The Cut A Round Tool (by Phillips Fiber Art) creates up to 17" circles. The rule of 1" applies to all these tools as well. The background circle is always cut 1" smaller than the circle that is being placed into it.

You can always use an old-fashioned compass and draw the circle onto paper. Then use the paper as a pattern on the fabric and either trace the circle or cut around the paper. You can certainly draw with the compass directly on the fabric. It would also work to make a circle on freezer paper. Cut a circle out and then iron it on to the fabric. Cut around the freezer paper. Use caution when doing this as to not stretch the circle when removing the freezer paper.

It may be tempting to trace a round object. Just be careful when doing this because circles can be distorted, and you may have a hard time trying to measure 1" larger or smaller than your object.

For this book, I used the Cut A Round Tool because I needed to cut larger circles. To do this, follow the manufacturer's directions on folding the fabric and cutting.

Sewing the Curves

There are special sewing machine presser feet made for sewing curves. These can be useful, but you can certainly sew the circles with a ¼" presser foot.

Marking Your Circle

1. Cut the set-in circle to the correct size.

2. Fold the set-in circle in half and press lightly with an iron. Make certain to use an up-and-down motion rather than a stroking motion to avoid distorting the bias edges.

3. Fold the set-in circle in half again so that it is quartered and press again.

4. Open the circle out. Mark the creases with pins.

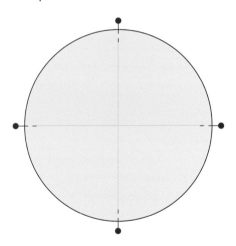

5. Fold the background in half and press. Fold it in half again so that it is quartered. Press.

6. Open out and mark the creases with pins.

7. Cut out the background circle 1" smaller than the circle to be set into it, using the creases to center the circle.

Sewing the Set-In Circle

From here on out, I will call the inside circle the *convex circle* and the background will be the *concave circle*. The convex circle always goes on top when sewing a circle into another. This is true for all curves. It may be tempting to put the concave on top because it seems easier to manipulate—*do not do this*. The concave circle has more stretch. It will become distorted.

1. Line up the pins that were placed. If you find that pins are in the way, which I often do, you can make a tiny little snip with your scissors (about ⅛") to mark where the crease is.

2. With the convex edge on the top and the concave under it, right sides together, match the edges.

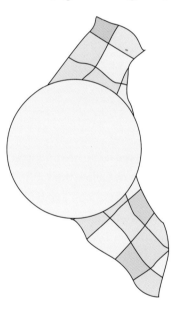

3. Use a ¼" presser foot and the needle-down setting on the sewing machine. As you begin sewing, keep the edges of the fabric together. Hold the convex circle at about a 45° angle relative to the throat plate of the sewing machine. The concave edge should lie flat next to the feed dogs.

4. Sew a ¼" seam allowance, holding the convex edge continuously up at a 45° angle.

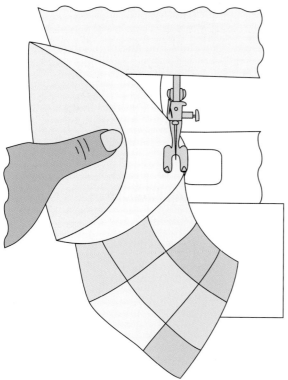

Hold the circle up at a 45° angle.

5. Evaluate as you're sewing to see if the next quarter markings will come together. Do not allow the fabrics to pucker or stretch. Use somewhat of a rolling technique with the convex circle. As you're holding it at this angle, envision that you are actually rolling it along the concave edge.

Tip   I love to sew using a round toothpick as a stiletto to help move the concave edge forward or to hold it so that the edges are together. Don't use a metal stiletto, which is too slippery and could cause injury if the needle hits it while you're sewing.

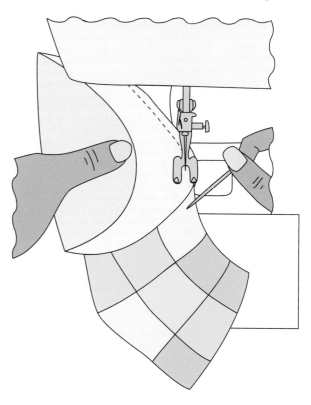

6. Remove pins as you come to them. Continue to sew around the circle until you come to the beginning.

Tip   Using the needle-down setting allows you to stop and take breaks. It is acceptable to lift the presser foot as often as needed and readjust your fabrics. Just make sure to hold the convex edge at an angle when sewing.

7. Pressing the seam allowance toward the inside circle gives an appliqué appearance. Pressing the seam allowance toward the background circle gives a reverse appliqué appearance.

THE QUILTS

So, here come the quilts! So much more scrappiness to love. Some of them use color progression; some do not. Have fun making them with your own scraps. Make them your personal walk down memory lane!

Frontal Boundaries

FINISHED BLOCK: 4″ × 4″ (380 blocks) • **FINISHED QUILT:** 68½″ × 97″

This quilt was made during one of our polar vortex weeks. The Midwest, particularly Wisconsin, can get mighty cold. This is not a typical temperature quilt. The inspiration for this quilt came on one particularly cold day from the map showing the temperatures across the country. I saved the photo to my computer and went to work immediately. This quilt uses my technique of color transitioning. When cutting the number of squares required for this quilt, make certain to read Transitioning Colors That Are Not Color Wheel Neighbors (page 21). Keep in mind that when you are cutting the colors specified, some of these need to be the actual color, with a few squares sprinkled in that contain both the color and the color that comes next in the quilt. Having a wide variety of scraps will add to the interest of this quilt.

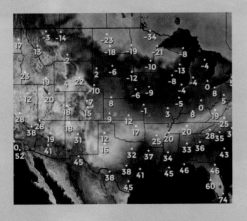

Materials

ASSORTED SCRAPS

Yellow-green: 1⅝ yards

Deep violet: 3¼ yards

Blue-violet (periwinkle): 4½ yards

Light blue-violet (light periwinkle): 1⅜ yards

Fuchsia: 2¼ yards

Pink: 1 yard

ADDITIONAL FABRIC

Binding: ¾ yard

Backing: 6 yards

OTHER SUPPLIES

Batting: 77″ × 105″

Tip When cutting squares, you may have extra left over at the end of the quilt. Because this quilt is made using blending of colors, it can be difficult to give an exact number of how many squares of each color to cut. Instructions are written so that there are more squares rather than fewer so that there will be enough. The cutting quantities are my best estimates of the number needed and may differ depending on the quilter's preferences of color selection and transitioning of color.

Cutting

Yellow-green: Cut 60 squares 5½″ × 5½″.

Deep violet: Cut 140 squares 5½″ × 5½″.

Blue-violet (periwinkle): Cut 190 squares 5½″ × 5½″.

Light blue-violet (light periwinkle): Cut 50 squares 5½″ × 5½″.

Fuchsia: Cut 90 squares 5½″ × 5½″.

Pink: Cut 30 squares 5½″ × 5½″.

Binding: Cut 9 strips 2½″ × width of fabric.

Making the Triangle Blocks

All seam allowances are ¼″ unless otherwise noted. Follow the arrows for the pressing direction.

1. For the yellow-green triangle blocks, select 2 matching pairs of 2 yellow-green squares.

2. Place 2 different yellow-green squares right sides together.

3. Draw a diagonal line on the top square from one corner to the opposite corner.

4. Stitch ¼″ on both sides of the line.

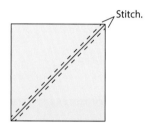

5. Cut along the line to yield 2 half-square triangle units. Press seam allowances as shown.

6. Place a half-square triangle on top of one of the remaining yellow-green squares, right sides together, and center the half-square triangle unit.

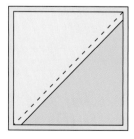

7. Draw a line on the half-square triangle unit perpendicular to the seam from one corner to the opposite corner.

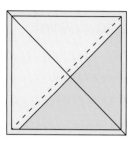

8. Stitch ¼″ on both sides of the line.

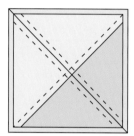

9. Cut along the line. Press the seam allowances as shown.

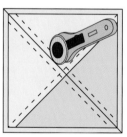 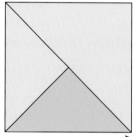 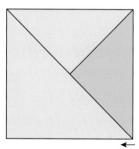

10. Using the remaining yellow-green square, repeat Steps 6–9 with the second of the 2 half-square triangle units created in Step 5 to complete a set of 4 blocks.

11. Center a 4½″ square template over the blocks and square them to 4½″ × 4½″.

12. Repeat Steps 1–11 to make 24 of these blocks, or more or less depending on your gradation preference.

NOTE *To produce a more varied block, one that has greater variation in scraps, follow the instructions for Making the Transition Blocks (below). This method will be used when the actual gradation is needed when moving from one color to the next.*

Making the Transition Blocks

Any time you need to transition from one color to another the blocks will be constructed the same way. However, the fabrics used will change. To make a transition block you will use the main color and then the color that you are transitioning to.

1. For the yellow-green / deep violet transition blocks, select 2 different yellow-green squares and 2 different deep violet squares.

2. Refer to Making the Triangle Blocks, Steps 2–5 (previous page) to make 2 half-square triangle units, using a yellow-green square and a deep violet square.

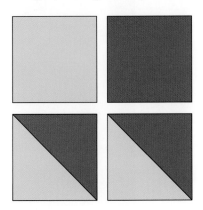

3. Combine 1 half-square triangle unit from Step 2 with a yellow-green square and 1 half-square triangle unit with a deep violet square.

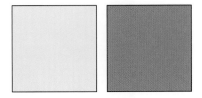

4. Refer to Making the Triangle Blocks, Steps 6–11 (previous page) to make 4 combined yellow-green / deep violet blocks.

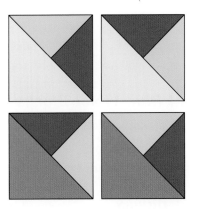

5. Repeat Steps 1–4 to make 32 of these blocks.

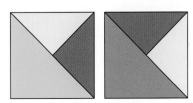

The number of each of these blocks can be fluid, depending on how you transition your blocks.

NOTE *You may need to make more or less of these blocks depending on how you transition your colors. You may also need to make more blocks that have 2 yellow-green triangles and 1 deep violet triangle, or more that have 2 deep violet triangles and 1 yellow-green triangle. This can only be determined by how you are transitioning your colors.*

Making the Remaining Blocks

Deep Violet Blocks

Refer to Making the Triangle Blocks, Steps 2–11 (page 30) to make 68 scrappy deep violet blocks, using 2 pairs of matching deep violet squares for each set of 4 blocks.

Deep Violet/Blue-Violet Blocks

Refer to Making the Transition Blocks, Steps 1–4 (page 31) to make 20 combined deep violet / blue-violet transition blocks, using 2 different deep violet and 2 different blue-violet squares for each set of 4 blocks.

Blue-Violet Blocks

Refer to Making the Triangle Blocks, Steps 2–11 (page 30) to make 108 scrappy blue-violet blocks, using 2 pairs of matching blue-violet squares for each set of 4 blocks.

Blue-Violet/Light Blue-Violet Blocks

Refer to Making the Transition Blocks, Steps 1–4 (page 31) to make 24 combined blue-violet / light blue-violet transition blocks, using 2 different blue-violet and 2 different light blue-violet squares for each set of 4 blocks.

Light Blue-Violet Blocks

Refer to Making the Triangle Blocks, Steps 2–11 (page 30) to make 16 scrappy light blue-violet blocks, using 2 pairs of matching light blue-violet squares for each set of 4 blocks.

Light Blue-Violet/Fuchsia Blocks

Refer to Making the Transition Blocks, Steps 1–4 (page 31) to make 20 combined light blue-violet / fuchsia transition blocks, using 2 different light blue-violet and 2 different fuchsia squares for each set of 4 blocks.

Fuchsia Blocks

Refer to Making the Triangle Blocks, Steps 2–11 (page 30) to make 44 scrappy fuchsia blocks, using 2 pairs of matching fuchsia squares for each set of 4 blocks.

Fuchsia/Pink Blocks

Refer to Making the Transition Blocks, Steps 1–4 (page 31) to make 12 combined fuchsia/pink transition blocks, using 2 different fuchsia and 2 different pink squares for each set of 4 blocks.

Pink Blocks

Refer to Making the Triangle Blocks, Steps 2–11 (page 30) to make 12 scrappy fuchsia blocks, using 2 pairs of matching pink squares for each set of 4 blocks.

Cutting the Setting Squares

NOTE *After this quilt is quilted, the setting squares are trimmed to triangles. Starting with squares allows for a nonbias edge on the quilt while it is being constructed.*

1. Determine what color the squares need to be to match the ends of the diagonal rows. Trim 54 squares to 4½″ × 4½″ to be the end squares.

2. Select 1 yellow-green square, 1 blue-violet square, and 2 fuchsia squares to be the corner squares. Trim to 4½″ × 4½″.

Constructing the Quilt

The blocks in this quilt are assembled "on point." It is necessary to have a design wall or a large area of floor so that the blocks can be laid out prior to sewing together. Make your transition from color to color as smooth as possible. Note that there may be more or fewer blocks of certain colors or certain combinations needed as you put your quilt together. This quilt is a very individualized process. Create more blocks as needed to enable you to finish this in the way that looks best to you. The patches on the ends are setting squares instead of setting triangles. This prevents the quilt from having wavy edges. After the quilt is quilted, you trim the squares to triangles.

1. Lay the blocks out in rows on point. Use the quilt photo (page 28) for reference.

2. Take frequent photos using a digital camera or smartphone during the process. Assess the quality of your layout based on the photos and arrange the blocks accordingly.

3. Stitch the blocks right sides together to make long diagonal rows, referring to the quilt photo.

4. The first diagonal row will have 1 block and 2 end squares with a pink corner square.

5. The second diagonal row will have 3 blocks with 2 end squares.

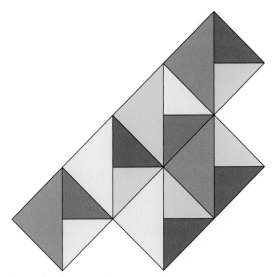

Example of on-point layout

6. The third diagonal row will have 5 blocks with 2 end squares.

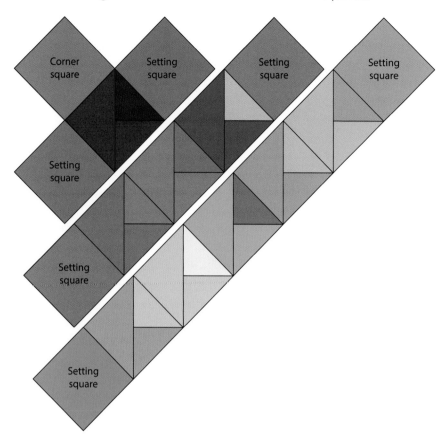

7. Continue in this manner until the twelfth row, which will have 23 blocks. The top square of this diagonal row will form the upper right corner of the quilt.

8. Sew the pink corner square to the upper right block of the row of 23, and then sew an end square to the lower block of the row of 23, referring to the quilt photo.

9. The thirteenth diagonal row will start one block below the previous row's top right block and will also have 23 blocks. Sew an end square to each end of the row.

10. Repeat Step 9 to make 3 more rows. The seventeenth row has an end block at the top and a yellow-green corner block at the end. This forms the lower left corner of the quilt.

11. The next diagonal row will have 21 blocks with 2 end squares. Continue decreasing blocks until the lower right corner has 1 block with 2 end squares on the ends, and a blue corner square.

12. Sew the diagonal rows together.

Finishing the Quilt

1. Layer the quilt top, batting, and backing.

2. Quilt the quilt using your favorite method.

3. Trim the edges of the quilt straight.

4. Bind the quilt using your favorite method.

Quilt assembly

True North

FINISHED BLOCK: 8″ × 8″ (112 blocks) • **FINISHED QUILT:** 91″ × 91″

This quilt has the feel of a compass. The blocks point in two different directions and form a latticework throughout the whole quilt. There is a color transition as the red moves to pink and then to gold and finally to mint. The blocks are made using my signature and favorite cutting technique.

The amounts of each color to be cut are a close count of the colors that I used. The numbers are larger than what you may need. By doing this, I am allowing you to add more or less of a color so that you can make interesting transitions. You may choose to incorporate different amounts of each color, and you may interpret your colors differently. In this way, you won't come up short. It is important to read Transitioning Colors That Are Not Color Wheel Neighbors (page 21) before making this quilt. There will be leftover pieces that will be all ready for the next quilt, *Argyle Sweater* (page 42).

Materials

ASSORTED SCRAPS

Red: 1⅜ yards

Deep pink: 1⅛ yards

Pink: 1¾ yards

Pink-and-gold prints: 1¼ yards

Gold: 3⅛ yards

Gold-and-mint prints: ¾ yard

Mint: 3⅛ yards

ADDITIONAL FABRIC

White solid: 9¾ yards

Binding: ⅞ yard

Backing: 8¼ yards

OTHER SUPPLIES

Batting: 99″ × 99″

Cutting

Red
- Cut 30 squares 5½″ × 5½″.
- Cut 24 squares 4½″ × 4½″.

Deep pink
- Cut 28 squares 5½″ × 5½″.
- Cut 10 squares 4½″ × 4½″.

Pink
- Cut 46 squares 5½″ × 5½″.
- Cut 30 squares 4½″ × 4½″.

Pink-and-gold prints
- Cut 18 squares 5½″ × 5½″.
- Cut 36 squares 4½″ × 4½″.

Gold
- Cut 86 squares 5½″ × 5½″.
- Cut 54 squares 4½″ × 4½″.

Gold-and-mint prints
- Cut 12 squares 5½″ × 5½″.
- Cut 12 squares 4½″ × 4½″.

Mint
- Cut 30 squares 5½″ × 5½″.
- Cut 122 squares 4½″ × 4½″.

White solid
- Cut 250 squares 5½″ × 5½″.
- Cut 256 squares 4½″ × 4½″.

Binding: Cut 10 strips 2½″ × width of fabric.

Making the Blocks

All seam allowances are ¼″ unless otherwise noted. Follow the arrows for the pressing direction. There are two methods for making the Keystone units; choose one below.

Making the Keystone Units

OPTION 1: STACKING METHOD

1. Layer 2 colored 5½″ × 5½″ squares with 2 white 5½″ × 5½″ squares and align them in a stack.

2. Follow Making the Keystone Block, Steps 3–10 (pages 10–13).

3. Place a 4½″ template in the upper corner of the rectangles, and square each unit to 4½″ × 4½″.

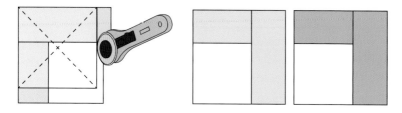

4. Set aside the units with colored squares and white rectangles to use in the *Argyle Sweater* quilt (page 42), if desired.

5. Skip to Making the Appliqué Units (next page).

OPTION 2: TRADITIONAL METHOD

1. From 2 stacked colored 5½″ × 5½″ squares, subcut 2 rectangles 2″ × 5½″, 2 rectangles 2″ × 3½″, and 2 squares 3½″ × 3½″.

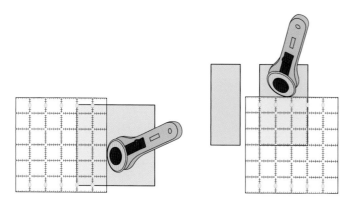

2. Repeat Step 1 with 2 white 5½″ × 5½″ squares.

3. Set aside the white rectangles and the colored squares.

4. With right sides together, stitch a colored 2″ × 3½″ rectangle to each white 3½″ × 3½″ square. Press the seam allowances toward the colored rectangles.

5. With right sides together, stitch a colored 2″ × 5½″ rectangle to the right side of each square/rectangle unit sewn in Step 4.

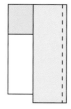

6. Press the seam allowances toward the colored rectangles.

7. Place a 4½″ template in the upper corner of the rectangles, and square the units to 4½″ × 4½″.

8. Repeat Steps 4–7 with the pieces set aside in Step 3 to use in the *Argyle Sweater* quilt, if desired.

Making the Appliqué Units

1. Fold a colored 4½″ × 4½″ square in half along the diagonal, right sides together.

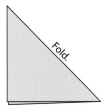

2. Stitch ¼″ along one edge. Clip the corner.

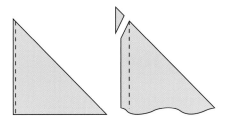

3. Finger-press the seam allowance to one side. Turn right side out. Press so that the seam allowance is centered.

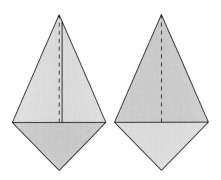

4. Machine appliqué this cone-shaped piece to a white 4½″ × 4½″ square using your favorite appliqué method. I used a blind hem stitch.

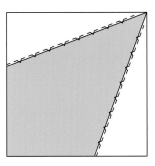

Block Assembly

1. Sew an appliqué unit to a keystone unit, right sides together and oriented as shown. Press the seam allowance to one side.

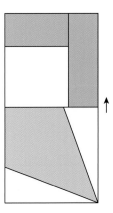

2. Repeat Step 1 to make a second pair.

3. Rotate 1 pair and stitch the 2 pairs together as shown, nesting the seam allowances. Press the seam allowance to one side.

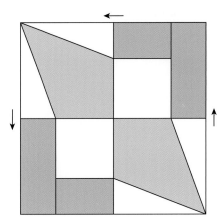

NOTE *You might want to make 10 blocks of each of the following colors and combinations, and begin laying them out. Then you can determine how many more of each of the various combination blocks you will need to make.*

4. Repeat Steps 1–3 to make the following:

11–14 blocks with red keystone units and red appliqué units

11–12 transition blocks with red keystone units and pink appliqué units
(*In some of these blocks, be sure to use some of the deep pinks that were cut.*)

12–13 blocks with pink keystone units and pink appliqué units

23–27 blocks with pink-and-gold print keystone units and pink-and-gold print appliqué units
(*Make certain to use predominantly gold and predominantly pink scraps in some of these blocks.*)

18–21 blocks with gold keystone units and gold appliqué units

12–13 blocks with gold-and-mint print keystone units and gold appliqué units

25–28 blocks with gold keystone units and mint appliqué units

Making the Setting Units

NOTE *The quilt blocks are set on point, which necessitates setting triangles. I never send my quilts to the quilter with setting triangles for fear of them being stretched. Rather, I use squares, and then after the quilt is quilted, I trim them off to make triangles. This creates stability in the bordering blocks so that minimal stretching can occur.*

1. Stitch a white 4½″ × 4½″ square to a mint 4½″ × 4½″ square. Press the seam allowance toward the mint square.

2. Stitch a mint 4½″ × 4½″ square to the white square in the unit from Step 1. Press the seam allowance toward the mint square.

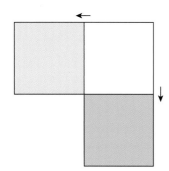

3. Repeat Steps 1 and 2 for a total of 32 setting units.

Constructing the Quilt

NOTE *It is especially important to have a design wall or floor space to lay out this quilt. The color positioning will be the most fun part. Be sure to give yourself enough room and time to lay the blocks out to get the most from your color transition.*

1. Lay the blocks out for the entire quilt using the quilt photo (page 36) as your guide.

2. *Row 1:* Beginning in the upper right corner, stitch 2 setting units right sides together. Press the seam allowance as shown.

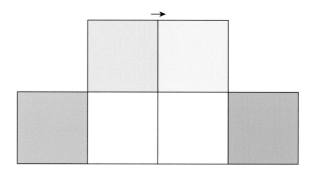

3. Lay each setting unit right sides together with a block, keeping the appliqué units oriented toward the center. Stitch each pair together.

4. *Row 2:* Stitch 2 units from Step 3 together. Press the seam allowance as shown.

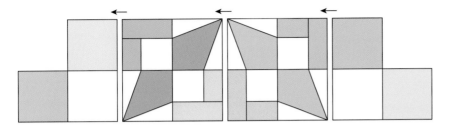

5. *Rows 3–8:* Continue in this manner, alternating the direction of the appliqué units and adding the setting units at the end of each row, until there is a row with 14 blocks and 1 setting unit on each end. (This will be the eighth row.) Press the seam allowances in the opposite direction for each row. Use the quilt photo (page 36) for reference.

6. *Row 9:* Create the ninth row with 14 blocks and 1 setting unit on each end.

7. *Rows 10–16:* Continue to make rows, each time with 2 fewer blocks in each row and a setting unit on each end. Alternate the direction for pressing the seam allowances. The last row will be 2 setting units, just like the upper right corner in Step 2.

8. Sew the rows together.

Finishing the Quilt

1. Layer the quilt top, batting, and backing.

2. Quilt the quilt using your favorite method.

3. Trim the setting units so that they are triangles and the quilt is square.

4. Bind the quilt using your favorite method.

Argyle Sweater

FINISHED BLOCK: 8″ × 8″ • **FINISHED QUILT:** 74″ × 85½″

This quilt is completely made with the leftovers from the quilt *True North* (page 36). Add a background fabric and you have another quilt entirely! Of course, instructions are provided in case you want to do this without doing the other quilt first. It resembles an argyle sweater, and who doesn't love argyle?

VERSION 1: WITH *TRUE NORTH* LEFTOVERS

The keystone units left over from *True North* consist of a 3½″ × 3½″ colored square bordered by a white 2″ × 3½″ rectangle and a white 2″ × 5½″ rectangle.

Materials

Keystone units: 238 leftover keystone units from *True North* (There should be 250 units available.)

Gray: 3 yards

Binding: ¾ yard

Backing: 7 yards

Batting: 82″ × 94″

Cutting

Gray: Cut 23 strips 4½″ × width of fabric; subcut 180 squares 4½″ × 4½″.

Binding: Cut 9 strips 2½″ × width of fabric.

Making the Units

All seam allowances are ¼" unless otherwise noted. Follow the arrows for the pressing direction.

Creating Unit A

1. Make a four-patch unit of gray 4½" × 4½" squares by sewing 2 pairs of gray squares right sides together. Press the seam allowances in alternate directions.

2. Stitch the 2 pairs together, allowing the seam allowances to nest. Press the seam allowance as shown. Make 16.

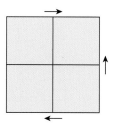

3. Set aside 2 four-patch units and label them unit A. These units belong in the upper right and lower left corners of the quilt.

4. You will use the other 14 gray four-patch units to create units B and C.

Creating Unit B

1. Using 2 of the four-patch units, add a gray 4½" × 4½" square to both sides of each four-patch unit. Press the seams as shown. Label these unit B.

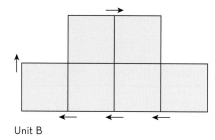

Unit B

2. Unit B belongs in the upper left and lower right corners of the quilt.

Creating Unit C

1. Using the 12 remaining four-patch units, stitch an additional gray 4½" × 4½" square to the upper right side of each four-patch, paying close attention to the orientation. Press the seam allowance of 6 units toward the small square.

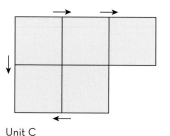

Unit C

2. For the last 6 units made in Step 1, press the seam allowance toward the four-patch.

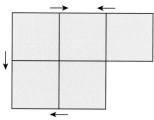

Unit C alternate

Sensational Quilts for Scrap Lovers

Creating Unit D

1. Make a four-patch unit using a keystone unit and 3 gray 4½" × 4½" squares. Pay close attention to the orientation of the keystone unit. Press the seam allowances as shown so that the seams nest.

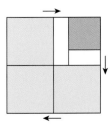

2. Add a gray 4½" × 4½" square to one side, making certain that the orientation is as shown. Press as shown. Label it unit D. Make 6 of unit D as shown.

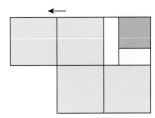

Unit D

3. Make 4 more of unit D, pressing the seam of the small square toward the four-patch unit.

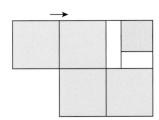

Unit D alternate

Creating Unit E

1. Make a four-patch unit using 4 keystone units, all in one color.

2. Press the seam allowances in opposite directions so that the seams nest. Label it unit E.

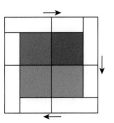

Unit E

3. Repeat Steps 1 and 2 for a total of 42 units. Keep the color the same in each unit.

Laying Out the Quilt

Prior to sewing the next group of blocks, the quilt will need to be laid out. Arrange all the E units, point to point according to color, in a way that you find pleasing. Leave empty spaces in between. Use the quilt photo (page 42) for reference.

Creating Unit F

1. Use your layout of E units as a guide for the color makeup of the F units.

2. Stitch a keystone unit to a gray 4½″ × 4½″ square. Press the seam allowance as shown. Make 2.

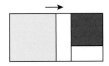

3. Stitch the pairs together, noting the orientation. Label this unit F. Make 30.

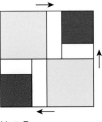

Unit F

Constructing and Finishing the Quilt

1. Using the quilt assembly diagram, add blocks A, B, C, and D, noting the placement of the alternate C and D blocks so that the seams nest.

2. Stitch the blocks together.

3. Alternate the pressed direction of the seam allowances as shown.

4. The edges of the rows will not be straight. Rather, they are zigzagged. This is so that the edges are not on the bias. It will keep the quilt from stretching when it is being quilted.

5. Layer and quilt the quilt using your favorite method.

6. Trim the quilt edges straight.

7. Bind the quilt using your favorite method.

Quilt assembly

VERSION 2: WITHOUT *TRUE NORTH* LEFTOVERS

Materials

ASSORTED SCRAPS

Gold: 1⅛ yards

Red: ½ yard

Pink: ⅞ yard, light to dark

Mint: ½ yard

ADDITIONAL FABRIC

Gray: 3 yards

White: 3¼ yards

Binding: ¾ yard

Backing: 7 yards

OTHER SUPPLIES

Batting: 82″ × 94″

Cutting

Gold: Cut 101 squares 3½″ × 3½″.

Red: Cut 41 squares 3½″ × 3½″.

Pink: Cut 68 squares 3½″ × 3½″.

Mint: Cut 28 squares 3½″ × 3½″.

Gray: Cut 23 strips 4½″ × width of fabric; subcut 180 squares 4½″ × 4½″.

White: Cut 56 strips 2″ × width of fabric; subcut 238 rectangles 2″ × 3½″ and 238 rectangles 2″ × 5½″.

Binding: Cut 9 strips 2½″ × width of fabric.

Making the Units

All seam allowances are ¼″ unless otherwise noted. Follow the arrows for the pressing direction.

1. With right sides together, stitch a white 2″ × 3½″ rectangle to a colored 3½″ × 3½″ square. Press the seam allowance toward the colored square.

2. With right sides together, stitch a white 2″ × 5½″ rectangle to the right side of the square/rectangle unit sewn in Step 1.

3. Press the seam allowance toward the colored square.

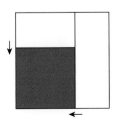

4. Repeat Steps 1–3 for the rest of the colored squares and white rectangles to make a total of 238 units.

5. Follow the Version 1 instructions for Making the Units (page 44) through Constructing and Finishing the Quilt (page 48).

Split Screens

This quilt uses the Keystone block format (page 10). I love to use this method. It's amazing how many different layout options this block can achieve. The cutting can be done using the stacking method or the traditional cutting method. If you stack and cut, the entire process is more fun and goes quickly. So, press those scraps and get to cutting!

Materials

ASSORTED SCRAPS

Navy: 2½ yards

Red: ½ yard

Yellow: ¾ yard

Gray: ½ yard

Medium blue: ½ yard

Green: ½ yard

Turquoise: ¾ yard

Tan: ½ yard

Pink: ½ yard

Purple: ½ yard

Coral: ½ yard

ADDITIONAL FABRIC

Binding: ⅝ yard

Backing: 3¼ yards

OTHER SUPPLIES

Batting: 57″ × 73″

Cutting

Navy: Cut 96 squares 5½″ × 5½″.

Red
• Cut 8 squares 5½″ × 5½″.
• Cut 4 squares 4½″ × 4½″.

Yellow
• Cut 16 squares 5½″ × 5½″.
• Cut 8 squares 4½″ × 4½″.

Gray
• Cut 8 squares 5½″ × 5½″.
• Cut 4 squares 4½″ × 4½″.

Medium blue
• Cut 8 squares 5½″ × 5½″.
• Cut 4 squares 4½″ × 4½″.

Green
• Cut 8 squares 5½″ × 5½″.
• Cut 4 squares 4½″ × 4½″.

Turquoise
• Cut 16 squares 5½″ × 5½″.
• Cut 8 squares 4½″ × 4½″.

Tan
• Cut 8 squares 5½″ × 5½″.
• Cut 4 squares 4½″ × 4½″.

Pink
• Cut 8 squares 5½″ × 5½″.
• Cut 4 squares 4½″ × 4½″.

Purple
• Cut 8 squares 5½″ × 5½″.
• Cut 4 squares 4½″ × 4½″.

Coral
• Cut 8 squares 5½″ × 5½″.
• Cut 4 squares 4½″ × 4½″.

Binding: Cut 7 strips 2½″ × width of fabric.

SUBCUTTING THE KEYSTONE UNITS

There are two methods for cutting the keystone units; choose one below.

Option 1: Using the stacking method

1. Align 2 navy 5½" × 5½" squares with 2 squares 5½" × 5½" of another color in one stack.

2. Follow Making the Keystone Block, Steps 3–8 (pages 10 and 11), to subcut:

> 4 rectangles 2" × 5½"
> (2 of navy and 2 of the other color)
>
> 4 rectangles 2" × 3½"
> (2 of navy and 2 of the other color)
>
> 4 squares 3½" × 3½"
> (2 of navy and 2 of the other color)

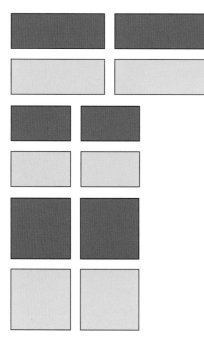

3. Repeat Steps 1 and 2 to subcut each set of 4 of the 5½" × 5½" squares, keeping the same colors together.

4. Skip to Making the Blocks (next page).

Option 2: Using the traditional method

For each of the 11 colors of 5½" × 5½" squares in the Cutting list (page 51), stack 2 squares and subcut:

> 2 rectangles 2" × 5½"
>
> 2 rectangles 2" × 3½"
>
> 2 squares 3½" × 3½"

Keep the same colors together.

Making the Blocks

All seam allowances are ¼" unless otherwise noted. Follow the arrows for the pressing direction.

For Steps 1–5, refer to Making the Keystone Block (page 10).

1. Stitch a navy 2" × 3½" rectangle to a turquoise 3½" × 3½" square. Press the seam allowance toward the navy.

2. Stitch a navy 2" × 5½" rectangle to the right side of the unit in Step 1. Press the seam allowance toward the navy. Label as unit A.

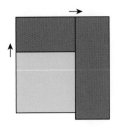

3. Square the unit A to 4½" × 4½" using the 4½" template. Make certain to place the template to capture the most of the 3½" square.

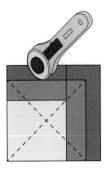

4. Repeat Steps 1–3 to make 8 A units.

5. Repeat Steps 1–3, but using turquoise rectangles and navy squares. They are the opposite of unit A. Make 4 and label these unit B.

8 unit A blocks

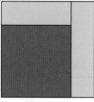

4 unit B blocks

6. Set aside any remaining cut squares and rectangles for another project.

7. Stitch 2 B units together in mirror image. Note the orientation. Press the seam allowance in the direction shown. Make 2.

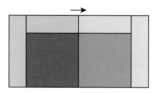

8. Stitch together the units created in Step 7, nesting the seam allowances to create a four-patch.

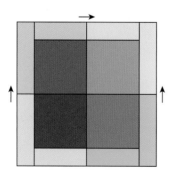

9. Stitch 2 A units together in mirror image.

10. Repeat Step 9 for a total of 4 pairs of unit A.

11. Stitch a 4½″ × 4½″ turquoise square to both ends of a unit A. Make 2.

12. Assemble the block.

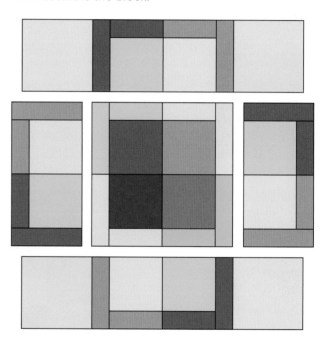

13. Repeat Steps 1–12 to make a total of 12 blocks, substituting each of the other colors for the turquoise in the first block.

Constructing the Quilt

1. Arrange the blocks so that the colors are pleasing to you.

2. Sew the blocks into 4 rows of 3 blocks each.

3. Sew the rows together.

Finishing the Quilt

Layer, quilt, and bind the quilt using your favorite method.

Precious Metals

FINISHED BLOCK: 5″ × 10″ • **FINISHED QUILT:** 60½″ × 70½″

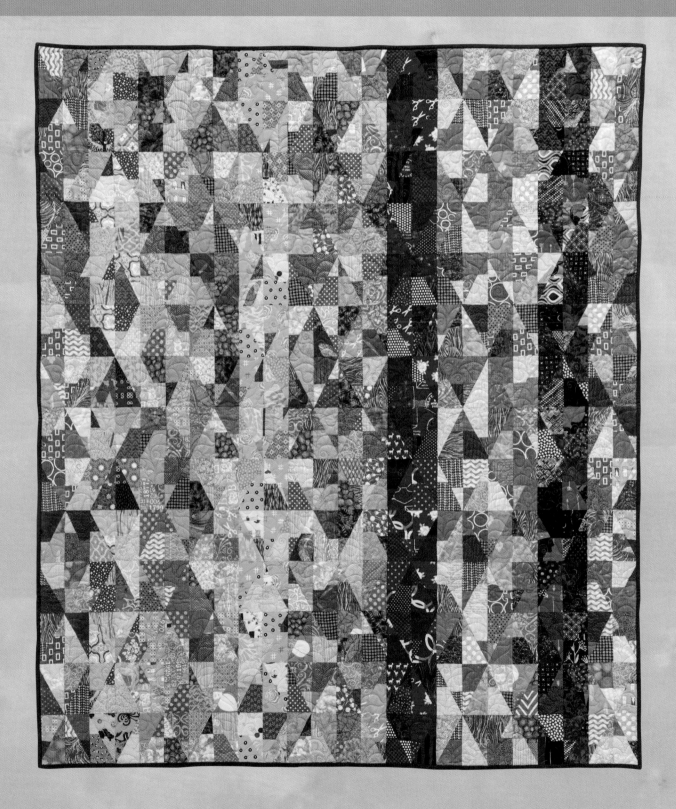

This quilt definitely has the "wow" factor. It looks terribly complicated, yet it couldn't be easier. If you don't have enough of your own gray scraps, you're going to have to appeal to your quilting besties or your quilt guild for help. You probably have a collection that you've started of gray fabric, so you can borrow a bit from your own uncut stash too. One of the best things about this quilt is that the effect is an overall one, and you don't have to be too careful about matching points. You will be working with bias edges in the course of this quilt, so be careful not to stretch them. Don't use your iron like a rolling pin. Press up and down.

When you see the number of squares that are needed from each color it can be a little daunting. Do not let this deter you! My suggestion would be to cut enough for one column, sew it, and then cut some more. That will make the process so much more fun.

Materials

ASSORTED SCRAPS

Gray prints: 4⅛ yards

Red prints: ¾ yard

Gold prints: ¾ yard

Turquoise prints: ¾ yard

Purple prints: ¾ yard

ADDITIONAL FABRIC

Binding: ⅝ yard

Backing: 4 yards

OTHER SUPPLIES

Batting: 69″ × 69″

Cutting

Gray prints: Cut 448 squares 3½″ × 3½″.

Red prints: Cut 56 squares 3½″ × 3½″.

Gold prints: Cut 56 squares 3½″ × 3½″.

Turquoise prints: Cut 56 squares 3½″ × 3½″.

Purple prints: Cut 56 squares 3½″ × 3½″.

Binding: Cut 8 strips 2½″ × width of fabric.

Making the Gray Blocks

All seam allowances are ¼″ unless otherwise noted. Follow the arrows for the pressing direction.

NOTE *Remember, the building blocks of this quilt are actually rectangular.*

1. Stitch 2 gray print 3½″ × 3½″ squares together. Press the seam allowance to one side. Make 2.

2. Lay the 2 sets of squares right sides together, turning one so that the seam allowances nest.

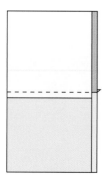

3. Stitch on both sides of the layered rectangles.

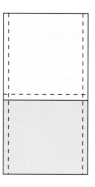

4. Place a quilting ruler diagonally across the rectangle, from the upper right corner to the lower left corner and cut along the ruler.

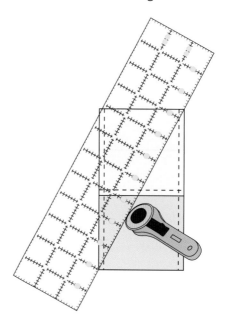

5. Open out the triangles. Press the seam allowances in the opposite direction so that they nest.

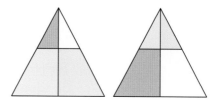

6. Repeat Steps 1 and 2. Do *not* stitch along the sides of these rectangles.

7. Place the quilting ruler diagonally across the stacked rectangles, from the upper right corner to the lower left corner and cut along the ruler.

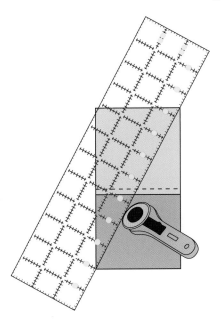

8. Open out the resulting triangles.

9. Place 2 triangles from Step 8 at the sides of a triangle from Step 5 along the long bias edges. The right-angle corners should be at the upper left and upper right.

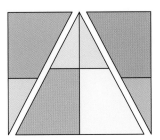

10. Stitch the triangles together and press the seam allowances outward. Make 2.

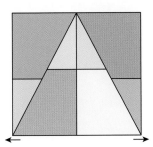

11. Place a 5½" template over a unit with the top ¼" line on the point of the center triangle and center the template.

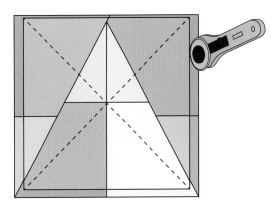

12. Cut around the template to square the unit.

13. Repeat Steps 1–12 to make 112 gray square units.

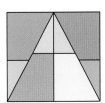

Make 112.

14. Select a pair of gray square units and turn the units so that they are mirror image of each other.

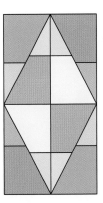

15. Place right sides together and stitch across the edge with the wide triangle base.

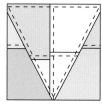

16. Press the seam allowance open.

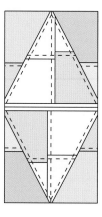

17. Repeat Steps 14–16 to make 48 gray rectangle blocks. The 16 remaining gray square units are added to each end of the gray columns.

Sewing the Gray Columns

1. Stitch a square unit to a rectangle block, orienting them as shown. Press the seam allowance open. Make 2.

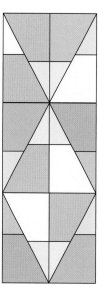

2. Stitch 4 rectangle blocks end to end along the short edges and press the seam allowances open.

3. Stitch the end units from Step 1 to the ends of the rectangle strips sewn in Step 2.

4. Repeat Steps 1–3 to make 8 gray rows. Use the quilt photo (page 60) for reference.

Making the Colored Blocks

Repeat Making the Gray Blocks, Steps 1–17 (pages 58–60), to make 7 rectangle blocks of each color.

Sewing the Colored Columns

1. Stitch the rectangle blocks end to end along the short ends and press the seam allowances open.

2. Repeat for all the colors.

Constructing the Quilt

1. Arrange the columns in order. Use the quilt photo for reference.

2. Stitch the columns together. Press the seam allowances to one side.

Finishing the Quilt

Layer, quilt, and bind the quilt using your favorite method.

Sleepy Tiny Tepee Town

FINISHED QUILT: 62½" × 78"

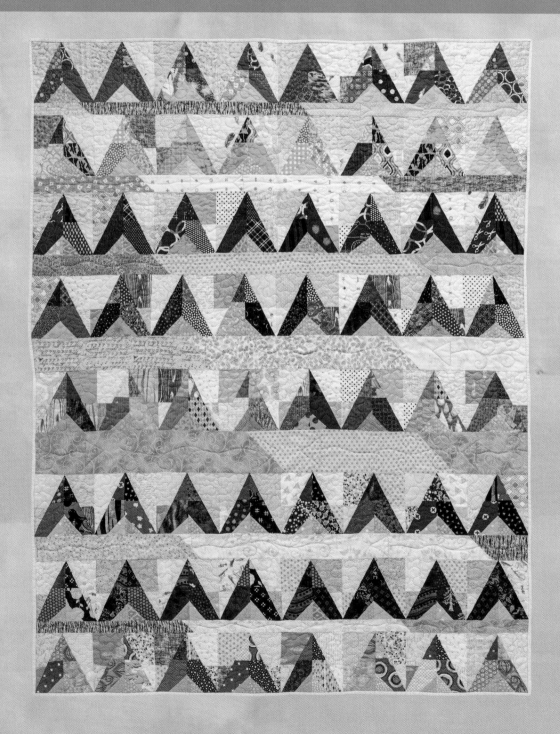

This quilt harkens back to scouting campgrounds and happy camping days. The tent flaps are sewn with a wonky technique to make them look more natural. You will rip through your scrap stash with this quilt.

NOTE *There are bias edges on this quilt—so imagine handling a delicate piecrust!*

Materials

ASSORTED SCRAPS

Pink: 3/8 yard

Brown: 3/8 yard

Blue: 3/8 yard

Green: 3/8 yard

Purple: 3/8 yard

Red: 3/8 yard

Turquoise: 3/8 yard

Orange: 3/8 yard

Yellow: 1 3/8 yards

Beige and gray: 2 1/8 yards

White, light brown, and off-white: 1 1/2 yards of assorted prints in long strips 2"–5 1/2" wide and 20"–40" long

ADDITIONAL FABRIC

Binding: 5/8 yard

Backing: 4 7/8 yards

OTHER SUPPLIES

Batting: 71" × 86"

Cutting

Pink: Cut 16 squares 4 1/2" × 4 1/2".

Brown: Cut 16 squares 4 1/2" × 4 1/2".

Blue: Cut 16 squares 4 1/2" × 4 1/2".

Green: Cut 16 squares 4 1/2" × 4 1/2".

Purple: Cut 16 squares 4 1/2" × 4 1/2".

Red: Cut 16 squares 4 1/2" × 4 1/2".

Turquoise: Cut 16 squares 4 1/2" × 4 1/2".

Orange: Cut 16 squares 4 1/2" × 4 1/2".

Yellow: Cut 128 small squares of varying sizes from 2 1/2" × 2 1/2" to 3 1/2" × 3 1/2".

Beige and gray: Cut 128 squares 4 1/2" × 4 1/2".

White, light brown, and off-white

• Cut 3 strips 5 1/2" wide of varying lengths to equal 74".

• Cut 3 strips 4 1/2" wide of varying lengths to equal 72".

• Cut 3 strips 3 1/2" wide of varying lengths to equal 70".

• Cut 3 strips 3" wide of varying lengths to equal 69".

• Cut 3 strips 2 1/2" wide of varying lengths to equal 68".

• Cut 6 strips 2" wide of varying lengths to equal 2 strips 67".

Binding: Cut 8 strips 2 1/2" × width of fabric.

Making the Colorful Tepees

All seam allowances are ¼" unless otherwise noted. Follow the arrows for the pressing direction.

1. Stitch 2 pink 4½" × 4½" squares together. Press the seam allowance to one side.

2. Lay a yellow square in the lower right corner of one of the squares, and a yellow square in the upper left corner of the other square, right sides together.

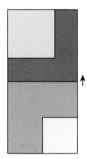

3. Stitch a diagonal line across the yellow squares, as shown, from upper right to lower left.

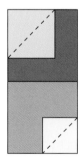

4. Fold the yellow squares along the stitching line and press.

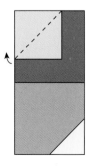

5. Trim the half of the yellow squares that are between the colored square and the top half of the yellow square.

6. Repeat Steps 1–5 in mirror image, pressing the seam allowances in the opposite directions so that they will nest.

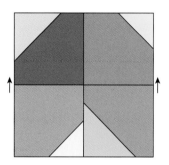

7. Place the 2 units right sides together, matching corners and edges. Stitch along the long edges.

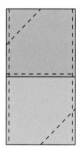

NOTE *The yellow triangles will not necessarily match at the points, as they are supposed to be different sizes to look like actual tent flaps.*

8. Place a quilting ruler diagonally on the squares, from the upper right corner to the lower left corner. Cut along the edge of the ruler with a rotary cutter.

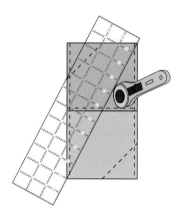

9. Open the triangles out and press the seam allowances open.

10. Repeat Steps 1–9 to create 8 tepees each of 8 color families.

Making the Background Tepees

Follow Making the Colorful Tepees, Steps 1–9 (previous page), using beige and gray squares and omitting the yellow squares to create 56 background tepees.

Making the Half-Tepees

1. Stitch 2 beige or gray 4½" × 4½" squares together and press the seam allowance to one side. Make 2.

2. Place the pairs of squares right sides together with seam allowances in opposite directions so that the seams nest.

3. Place a quilting ruler diagonally on the rectangles, from the upper right corner to the lower left corner. Cut along the ruler. You will have 4 half-tepees.

4. Repeat Steps 1–3 to make 16 half-tepees.

Sewing the Rows

1. Stitch a half-tepee to a colorful tepee as shown. Match the edges. The point of the colorful tepee should extend beyond the half-tepee by about ¼".

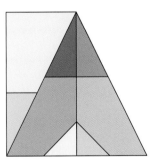

NOTE *The center seam of the colorful tepee will not match with the center seam of the half-tepee.*

2. Press the seam allowance toward the half-tepee.

3. Stitch a background tepee to the right side of the colorful tepee, with the background tepee upside down. The top point of the colorful tepee will extend about ¼" beyond the background tepee.

4. Press the seam toward the background tepee.

5. Stitch another colorful tepee to the right side of the background tepee.

6. Repeat Steps 3–5 across the row until you have used up all of one color of tepees; then sew a half-tepee to the end of the row.

7. Use the quilt photo (page 62) for reference.

8. Repeat Steps 1–7 for each color of tepees, creating a total of 8 rows.

Sewing the Strips and Constructing the Quilt

1. Place 2 strips 2″ wide right sides together at the ends, perpendicular to one another.

2. Draw a diagonal line from the upper left corner to the lower right corner.

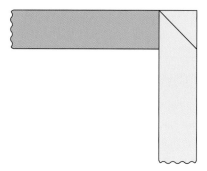

3. Stitch directly on the line.

4. Trim the corner.

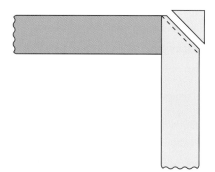

5. Open the strips out and press the seam allowance to one side.

6. Add a third 2″ strip, following Steps 1–5.

7. Cut the long strip to exactly 62½″.

8. Stitch the bottom of the orange row of tepees to the strip. Use the quilt photo for reference. Press the seam allowance toward the strip.

9. Repeat Steps 1–7 using the 2½″ strips.

10. Stitch the pieced 2½″ strip to the bottom of the turquoise tepees.

11. Continue in this manner, using the quilt photo for reference.

12. Stitch:

- the 3″ strip to the bottom of the red tepees
- the 4½″ strip to the bottom of the purple tepees
- the 5½″ strip to the bottom of the green tepees
- the 3½″ strip to the bottom of the blue tepees
- the 2″ strip to the bottom of the brown tepees

13. Sew all the rows together.

Finishing the Quilt

Layer, quilt, and bind the quilt using your favorite method.

The Knit Stitch

FINISHED BLOCK: 10″ × 5″ (60 blocks) • **FINISHED QUILT:** 50½″ × 60½″

One day I was looking at my knitting and I wondered, *What would a quilt block look like if it were made to resemble a knit stitch?* So, I put templates to work, cut up my scraps, and came up with this quilt. It makes the most of all the pieces that are cut. There is very little waste. If you stand back and look at it, it really does look like knitting.

Materials

ASSORTED SCRAPS

Red prints: 1⅛ yards

Dark pink prints: 1¼ yards

Light pink prints: ½ yard

Coral prints: ⅞ yard

White prints: 1¼ yards

ADDITIONAL FABRIC

Binding: ⅝ yard

Backing: 3⅜ yards

OTHER SUPPLIES

Batting: 59″ × 69″

Cutting

Red prints

• Cut 18 pairs of squares 5½″ × 5½″.

• Cut 2 squares 2½″ × 2½″.

Dark pink prints: Cut 22 pairs of squares 5½″ × 5½″.

Light pink prints: Cut 7 pairs of squares 5½″ × 5½″.

Coral prints: Cut 13 pairs of squares 5½″ × 5½″.

White prints: Cut 120 squares 3½″ × 3½″.

Binding: Cut 7 strips 2½″ × width of fabric.

Making the Blocks

All seam allowances are ¼″ unless otherwise noted. Follow the arrows for the pressing direction.

NOTE *Have a design wall or large table available when making this quilt. Fabric from one block is also used in the following block in the column. Therefore, you will need to know which fabric you are going to use for subsequent blocks when selecting fabrics.*

1. Arrange the pairs of 5½″ × 5½″ squares in 5 columns of 12 paired squares. The color variation from red to pink to coral can be referenced from the quilt photo (page 68).

2. Beginning with the first pair in the first column, lay a white print 3½″ × 3½″ square in the upper right corner of a red print 5½″ × 5½″ square, right sides together.

3. Draw a diagonal line from the upper left corner to the lower right corner of the white print square. Draw a second line ½″ above this line.

4. Stitch directly on the lines.

5. Trim the corner between the stitching lines. Set aside the half-square triangle.

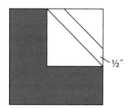

6. Press the white triangle out.

7. Open out the half-square triangle unit. Press the seam allowance toward the red.

8. Lay the half-square triangle unit on the lower left corner of the 5½″ × 5½″ square, right sides together. Note the orientation. Draw a diagonal line from the upper left corner to the lower right corner.

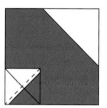

9. Stitch on the line. Trim the corner ¼″ from the stitching line. Press the triangle open. Save the solid red triangle that was trimmed off.

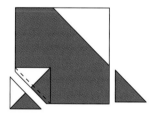

NOTE *This small triangle that you save will be the center triangle of the next block in the column.*

10. Place a red 2½″ × 2½″ leader square over the white triangle in the upper right corner.

11. Stitch across the square on the diagonal, from the upper left to the lower right corner. Trim ¼″ from the seam and press the square outward.

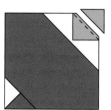 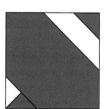

12. Square the block to 5½″ × 5½″.

13. Repeat Steps 2–12 with the second red 5½″ × 5½″ square, but this time in mirror image of the first block.

14. Repeat Steps 2–13 to make 60 sets of blocks, but use the lower cut corner from Step 9 instead of the leader square for all subsequent blocks.

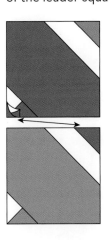

NOTE *The corners of the white squares will not necessarily line up perfectly. This is an element of the design, as it is meant to look imperfect.*

Constructing the Quilt

1. Sew each pair of blocks together. Press the seams in opposite directions.

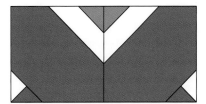

2. Make a total of 5 columns of 12 rectangular blocks each.

3. Stitch the columns together.

Finishing the Quilt

Layer, quilt, and bind the quilt using your favorite method.

Fractured
Four-Patch

FINISHED QUILT: 78½" × 93"

The complicated look of this quilt is part of its appeal. It's surprisingly simple. I used an adjacent color scheme with some neutrals in this quilt. It is pleasing to the eye, and a pleasure to make. You won't believe the simplicity.

Materials

ASSORTED SCRAPS

Dark turquoise: $1\frac{1}{8}$ yards

Medium turquoise: $1\frac{5}{8}$ yards

Green: $1\frac{1}{8}$ yards

Lime green: $\frac{5}{8}$ yard

Navy: $\frac{5}{8}$ yard

Blue: $1\frac{1}{8}$ yards

Brown: $\frac{5}{8}$ yard

Beige: $\frac{5}{8}$ yard

Cream: 1 yard

White: 1 yard

ADDITIONAL FABRIC

Binding: $\frac{7}{8}$ yard

Backing: $7\frac{1}{4}$ yards

OTHER SUPPLIES

Batting: 87″ × 101″

Cutting

COLORS

Dark turquoise: Cut 40 squares $5\frac{1}{2}$″ × $5\frac{1}{2}$″.

Medium turquoise: Cut 60 squares $5\frac{1}{2}$″ × $5\frac{1}{2}$″.

Green: Cut 40 squares $5\frac{1}{2}$″ × $5\frac{1}{2}$″.

Lime green: Cut 20 squares $5\frac{1}{2}$″ × $5\frac{1}{2}$″.

Navy: Cut 20 squares $5\frac{1}{2}$″ × $5\frac{1}{2}$″.

Blue: Cut 40 squares $5\frac{1}{2}$″ × $5\frac{1}{2}$″.

Brown: Cut 20 squares $5\frac{1}{2}$″ × $5\frac{1}{2}$″.

NEUTRALS

Beige: Cut 20 squares $5\frac{1}{2}$″ × $5\frac{1}{2}$″.

Cream: Cut 30 squares $5\frac{1}{2}$″ × $5\frac{1}{2}$″.

White: Cut 30 squares $5\frac{1}{2}$″ × $5\frac{1}{2}$″.

BINDING

• Cut 10 strips $2\frac{1}{2}$″ × width of fabric.

NOTE *When selecting the colored, scrappy blocks for this quilt, it is important to separate the lights, mediums, and darks and distribute them equally throughout the quilt. Don't worry as much about color placement as placement of lights and darks.*

Making the Triangles

All seam allowances are ¼" unless otherwise noted. Follow the arrows for the pressing direction.

1. Divide the colored squares into piles of lights, mediums, and darks.

NOTE *An excellent way to determine if your fabrics are light, medium, or dark is to use the black-and-white setting on a smartphone. Place several colored fabric pieces next to each other and look at them through the screen of the smartphone. Determine which ones look light and dark and separate those. The ones that are in between will be the mediums.*

2. Place 2 colored squares right sides together and stitch. Open out. Press the seam allowance to one side. Make 2.

3. Place the 2 pairs of squares right sides together with the seam allowances in opposite directions so that they nest.

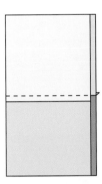

4. Stitch along both long edges.

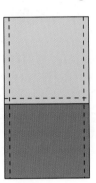

5. Place a quilting ruler from the upper right corner of the square to the lower left corner of the square and cut along the edge of the ruler with a rotary cutter.

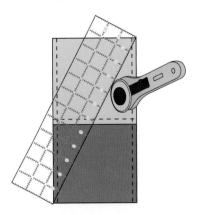

6. Open the triangles out. Press the seam allowances open.

7. Repeat Steps 2–6, using lights, mediums, and darks of the colored squares to make the triangles. Make 114 colored triangles.

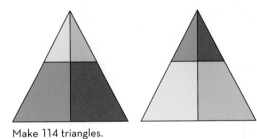

Make 114 triangles.

8. Repeat Steps 2–6, using the neutral squares. Make 36 neutral triangles.

Making the Half-Triangles

Making the Colored Half-Triangles

1. Repeat Making the Triangles, Steps 2 and 3 (page 75). Do not sew along the long edges.

2. Place a quilting ruler diagonally, from the upper right corner of the rectangle to the lower left corner of the rectangle.

3. Cut along the ruler with a rotary cutter.

4. Repeat Steps 1–3 to make 12 colored half-triangles.

Making the Neutral Half-Triangles

Using neutral squares, repeat Making the Colored Half-Triangles, Steps 1–3 (above). Make 8 neutral half-triangles.

Making the Diamonds

1. Place 2 colored triangles right sides together.

2. Stitch across the base of both triangles.

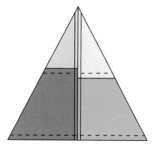

3. Open the triangles out to yield a diamond shape. Press the seam allowances open.

4. Repeat Steps 1–3 to make 40 diamonds total.

Constructing Rows 1, 3, and 5

1. Stitch a colored half-triangle to the upper left side of a colored diamond. Open out. Press the seam allowance open.

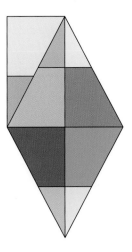

2. Stitch a colored half-triangle to the lower left side of the unit from Step 1. Open out. Press the seam allowance open.

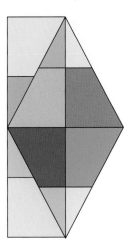

3. Stitch a neutral triangle to the upper right side of the unit created in Step 2. Press the seam allowance open.

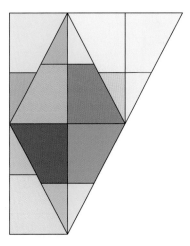

4. Repeat Steps 1–3 to make the end unit. Rotate it so the half-triangles are on the right side.

5. Stitch a neutral triangle to the lower left side of another colored diamond. Open out. Press the seam allowance open.

6. Stitch a colored triangle to upper right side of the neutral triangle/diamond combination in Step 5. Open out and press the seam allowance open. Label this unit M.

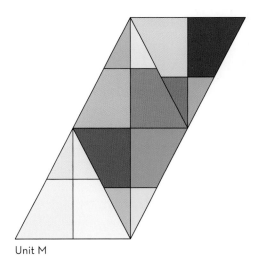

Unit M

7. Repeat Steps 5 and 6 to make 6 of unit M.

8. Stitch a unit M to the unit from Step 3 along the long edge with the neutral triangles.

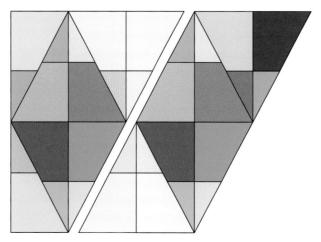

9. Rotate the next unit M to complete the colored hexagon and stitch to the unit from Step 8. Press the seam allowance open.

10. Sew the next unit M to the unit from Step 9. Use the quilt photo for reference.

11. Repeat Steps 9 and 10 to add the last 4 of unit M.

12. Complete the row by sewing the unit from Step 4 to the end.

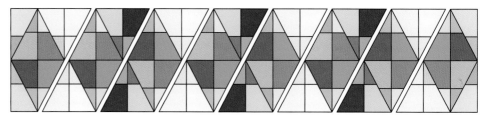

13. Repeat Steps 1–12 to make rows 3 and 5.

Constructing Rows 2 and 4

NOTE *Rows 2 and 4 are made in the same manner as rows 1, 3, and 5, with the exception of starting and ending the row with neutral half-triangles.*

1. Stitch a neutral half-triangle to a colored diamond on the upper left side of the diamond. Press the seam allowance open.

2. Stitch a neutral half-triangle to the lower left side of the diamond in Step 1. Open out and press the seam allowance open.

3. Stitch a colored triangle to the upper right side of the unit from Step 2. Open out and press the seam allowance open.

4. Repeat Steps 1–3 to make the end unit. Rotate the unit so that the half-triangles are on the right.

5. Repeat Construct Rows 1, 3, and 5, Steps 5 and 6 only (page 77), to make 6 of unit M.

6. Rotate a unit M to complete the colored hexagon and stitch to the unit from Step 3. Press the seam allowance open.

7. Stitch the next unit M to the unit from Step 6. Press the seam allowance open.

8. Repeat Steps 6 and 7 to add the last 4 of unit M.

9. Stitch the unit from Step 4 to the right end of the row. Press the seam allowance open.

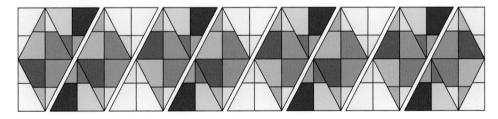

10. Repeat Steps 1–9 to make row 4.

Joining the Rows

1. Stitch the rows together in numerical order.

2. Press all the seam allowances down.

Finishing the Quilt

Layer, quilt, and bind the quilt using your favorite method.

Circle Gets the Square

FINISHED BLOCK: 21″ × 21″ (9 blocks) • **FINISHED QUILT:** 63½″ × 63½″

I wonder how many people actually remember that silly game show on TV called *Hollywood Squares*? That phrase "circle gets the square" kept popping up in my brain when I was making this quilt. I love piecing curves. I have become quite an expert in doing them because I love them. This is a little bit of a challenge, one that I hope can be made easier for you through my method of piecing curves.

Materials

ASSORTED SCRAPS AND ADDITIONAL FABRIC

Green: 2½ yards of assorted scraps

Yellow: 2 yards of assorted scraps + 1 fat quarter

Navy: ¾ yard of assorted scraps + 4 fat quarters

Red: ⅞ yard of assorted scraps + 4 fat quarters

Beige: ¾ yard of assorted scraps

Binding: ⅝ yard

Backing: 4 yards

OTHER SUPPLIES

Batting: 72" × 72"

Cutting

Green: Cut 260 squares 3½" × 3½".

Yellow

• Cut 201 squares 3½" × 3½".

• Cut 1 circle 17" in diameter

Navy

• Cut 65 squares 3½" × 3½".

• Cut 4 circles 17" in diameter

Red

• Cut 75 squares 3½" × 3½".

• Cut 4 circles 17" in diameter

Beige: Cut 65 squares 3½" × 3½".

Binding: Cut 7 strips 2½" × width of fabric.

Making the Background Blocks

All seam allowances are ¼" unless otherwise noted. Follow the arrows for the pressing direction.

1. Stitch a row of green squares that is 7 squares long. Press the seam allowances as shown.

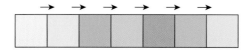

2. Repeat Step 1 for 7 rows total, alternating the pressing direction for the seam allowances.

3. Stitch the 7 rows together to make a green block.

4. Press the seam allowances in the direction of the pressing arrows.

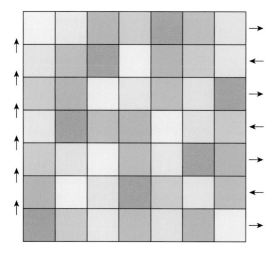

5. Repeat Steps 1–4 to make a total of 5 green blocks.

6. Repeat Steps 1–4, substituting the yellow squares to make 4 yellow blocks. Press the seam allowances in the opposite direction of the green blocks.

Making the Inside Circles

1. Stitch 5 red squares together in a row. Press the seam allowances as shown. Make 2.

2. Stitch a row of 5 squares together in this order: 2 red squares, 1 navy square, and 2 red squares. Press the seam allowances as shown. Make 2.

3. Stitch a center row of 5 squares consisting of 1 outer red square, 3 center navy squares, and 1 outer red square. Press the seam allowances as shown.

4. Stitch all the rows together to make a navy plus sign in the center of the red squares. Press the seam allowances as shown.

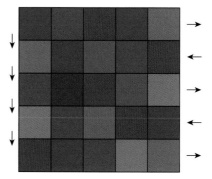

5. Repeat Steps 1–4 to make 9 units with the combined colors as shown in the quilt photo (page 80).

6. Fold a unit in half and press a crease. Without opening it out, fold again and press another crease.

7. Open it out. The center of the unit is now marked to allow for cutting a circle.

8. Cut 3 circles 15" in diameter from the red units.

9. Repeat Steps 6–8 to make the navy units.

10. Repeat Steps 6–8 to make the beige units.

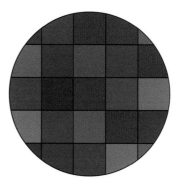

Making the Blocks

1. Follow Making the Inside Circles, Steps 6 and 7 (previous page), to find the center of a green block.

Tip   You may want to use a lightweight interfacing over the back of the background blocks if you feel you need to decrease stretching. This is optional.

2. Using the creases as a reference for centering, cut a 16" circle out of the green background block.

3. Repeat Steps 1 and 2 to cut a 16" circle from all the green background blocks and all the yellow background blocks.

4. Following the instructions in Let's Talk About Piecing Curves (page 23), set the 17" circles cut from the fat quarters into the background blocks. Use the quilt photo for reference in placing the colors.

5. Crease the blocks with the set-in circles a second time so that the center is identified.

6. Cut a 14" circle out of the circles made from the fat quarters, using the creases for the center reference.

7. Stitch the 15" circles with the plus signs into the 14" diameter openings, making certain to orient the plus signs so that they are all in the same direction. Continue to use the instructions from Let's Talk About Piecing Curves.

8. Press all seam allowances depending on the look you would like to achieve. The pressing of the seam allowances is referenced in Let's Talk About Piecing Curves.

Quilt Assembly

1. Arrange the blocks into rows and stitch them together, alternating the green and yellow blocks.

2. Use the quilt photo (page 80) for reference.

3. Press the seam allowances according to the pressing arrows. Stitch the rows together and press the seams in one direction.

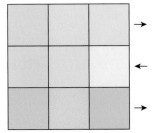

Finishing the Quilt

Layer, quilt, and bind the quilt using your favorite method.

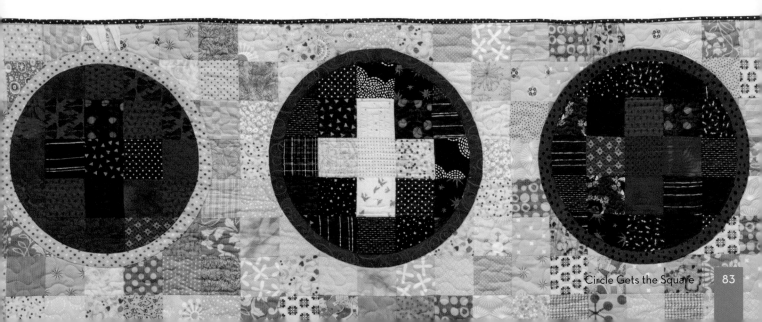

Aerial View

FINISHED BLOCK: 5¾" × 7" (100 blocks) • **FINISHED QUILT:** 58" × 70½"

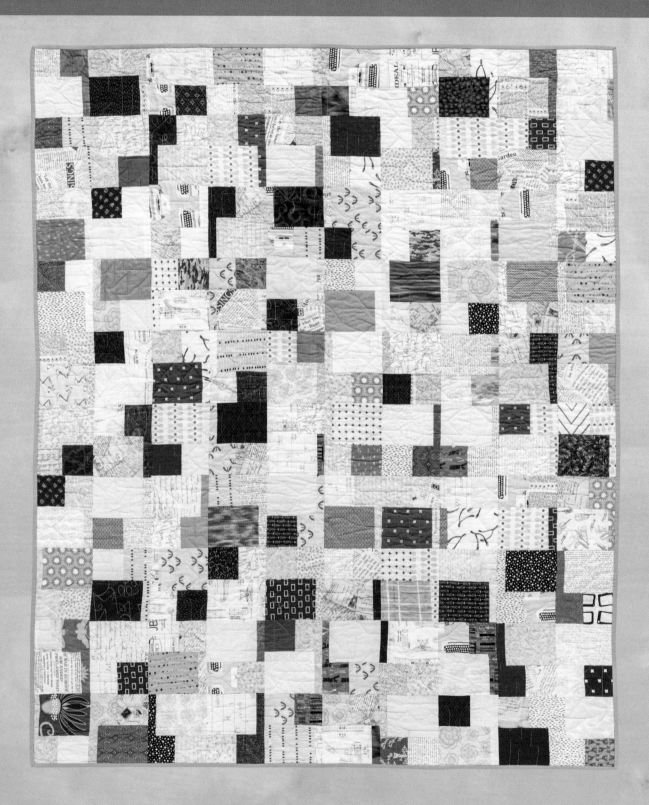

This quilt is totally crazy and totally fun. Once you get going, you'll be amazed at how many of your scraps you're going to use up. There's very little waste even though there's some trimming involved. You're going to have all your quilty friends exclaiming, "Where's the block?!"

Materials

ASSORTED SCRAPS

Cream prints: 3½ yards

Colored prints: 1⅞ yards

ADDITIONAL FABRIC

Binding: ⅝ yard

Backing: 3¾ yards

OTHER SUPPLIES

Batting: 66" × 79"

Cutting

Cream prints

• Cut 67 squares 5½" × 5½".

• Cut 67 squares 4½" × 4½".

• Cut 67 squares 3½" × 3½".

Colored prints

• Cut 33 squares 5½" × 5½".

• Cut 33 squares 4½" × 4½".

• Cut 33 squares 3½" × 3½".

Binding: Cut 7 strips
2½" × width of fabric.

Making the Blocks

All seam allowances are 1/4" unless otherwise noted. Follow the arrows for the pressing direction.

1. Stitch a 3½" × 3½" and a 5½" × 5½" cream print square to the either side of a colored 4½" × 4½" square. Press the seam allowance toward the outer edges.

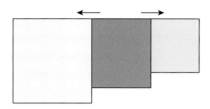

2. Repeat Step 1 to make 50 units, randomly choosing and placing cream and colored squares.

3. Repeat Step 1 to make 50 mirror image units, randomly choosing and placing cream and colored squares.

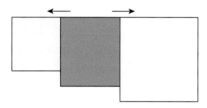

4. Place the unit on a cutting mat with a grid.

5. Measure 6¼" from the end to the center and make a mark.

6. Using the mat, a rotary cutter, and a ruler, make a straight cut down the center.

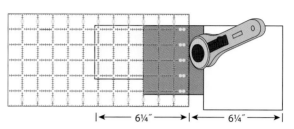

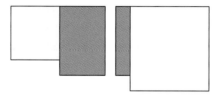

7. Place the right half-unit facedown on the left half-unit, matching the upper edges, and stitch the top seam.

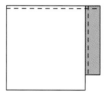

8. Open out and press the seam allowance toward the large square.

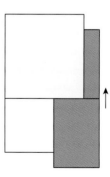

9. Trim the top and bottom even with the shorter sections to make a rectangle 6¼" × 7½".

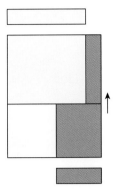

10. Repeat Steps 4–9 for all 100 blocks.

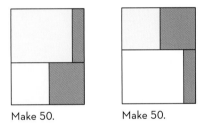

Make 50.   Make 50.

Tip In order to mix up the colors, you can mix and match the half-units with other half-units of the same orientation after making the cut in Step 6.

Making and Assembling the Rows

1. Arrange the blocks in rows of 10 along the 7½" edges so that the color combinations are pleasing to you.

2. Make sure to randomly place the blocks in their varying orientations. Half the blocks will be oriented one direction and half in the other direction, as the illustrations show in Making the Blocks, Step 10 (page 87).

3. Stitch the blocks together along the 7½" sides. Press the seam allowances in alternating directions per row.

4. Stitch together 10 rows of 10 blocks each.

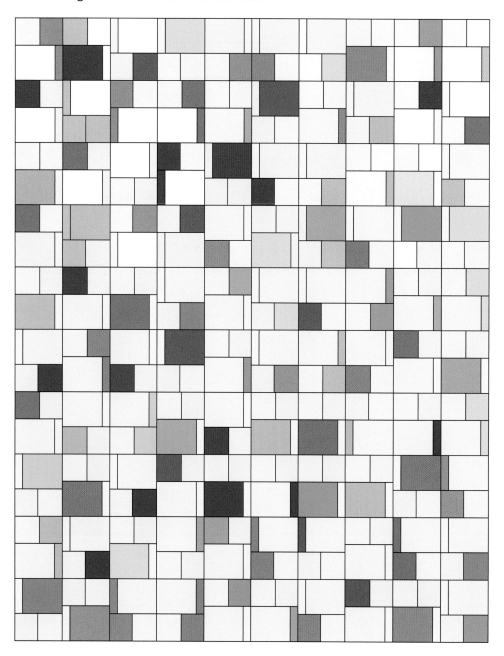

Finishing the Quilt

Layer, quilt, and bind the quilt using your favorite method.

Sunrise, Sunset

FINISHED QUILT: 77″ × 80½″

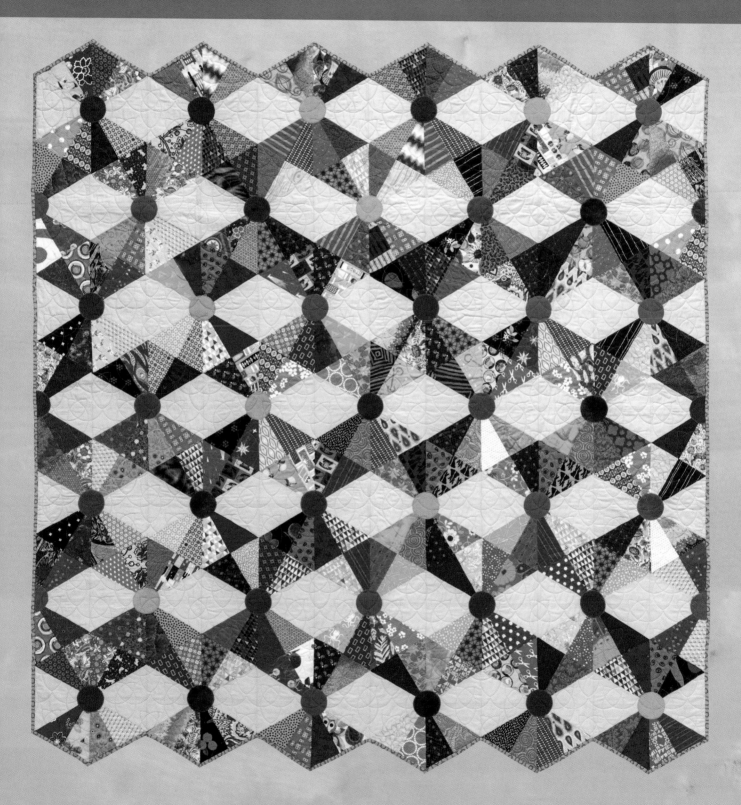

This quilt is another variation of a cutting method that I love to use. I have used it in many other quilts, and it has yet to fail me. Each time I use it and make any variation, it comes out beautifully. This one goes together particularly quickly.

I wanted to make a quilt using the colors of the sunrise and the sunset. The color theory used in this quilt is the complementary color scheme (page 17). I was a bit more liberal with this scheme, as I chose colors next to the orange and next to turquoise as well. I threw in some navy to give it some contrast, and it worked out well. When you look at a sunrise, it isn't just one color of orange, but a variation across the sky of orange, red, and sometimes magenta.

Materials

ASSORTED SCRAPS

Orange prints: 1 yard

Magenta prints: 1/3 yard

Pink prints: 2/3 yard

Navy prints: 1/3 yard

Turquoise prints: 1/3 yard

Yellow-orange prints: 1/3 yard

Orange-red prints: 1/2 yard

Red-orange prints: 1/2 yard

ADDITIONAL FABRIC

Gray solid: 2 yards

Binding: 3/4 yard

Backing: 7 1/8 yards

Orange felted wool: 1 fat quarter

Magenta felted wool: 1 fat quarter

Orange-yellow felted wool: 1 fat quarter

Red-orange felted wool: 1 fat quarter

OTHER SUPPLIES

Fusible interfacing: 3/4 yard of 20" wide

Batting: 85" × 89"

Tip When choosing your scraps, it is helpful to have with you a color wheel, such as the Essential Color Wheel Companion (by Joen Wolfrom, from C&T Publishing). Don't forget to include shades and tints of each of these colors as well. For example, a tint of orange is peach, and those scraps can be included too.

Cutting

Colored prints: Cut 168 squares 5½" × 5½".

Gray solid: Cut 84 squares 5½" × 5½".

Binding: Cut 9 strips 2½" × width of fabric.

Felted wools: Cut a total of 45 circles 3" in diameter.

Fusible interfacing: Cut 45 circles 3" in diameter.

Making the Wedges

All seam allowances are ¼" unless otherwise noted. Follow the arrows for the pressing direction.

1. Place 2 colored squares right sides together.

2. Make a mark 1³/₁₆" in from the upper right corner and 1³/₁₆" in from the lower left corner.

3. Connect the marks with a quilting ruler and cut along the ruler with a rotary cutter.

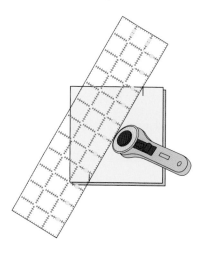

4. Move the stacks apart, but do not separate the stacked pieces that are cut.

5. Stitch along the long straight edge using a chain piecing method.

6. Open the pieces out and press the seams open.

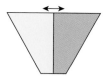

7. Repeat Steps 1–6 to make 168 colored print wedges.

8. Follow Steps 1–6 to make 84 gray solid wedges.

Making the Half-Hexagons

1. Stitch colored print wedges to both sides of a gray wedge. Press the seam allowances open. This will yield a half-hexagon.

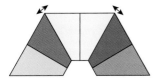

2. Repeat Step 1 to make 84 half-hexagons.

3. Stitch the half-hexagons together along the colored print edges. Press the seam allowance open.

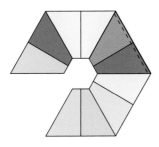

4. Repeat Step 3 until you have a column of 7 half-hexagons with the center of the hexagon in alternating directions.

NOTE *There will be half-hexagons in the very first column of the quilt that remain half-hexagons. This will also be the case for the very last column. Use the quilt photo (page 90) for reference.*

5. Repeat Steps 3 and 4 to make 12 columns.

Preparing the Circles

1. Fuse the interfacing circles to the backs of the felted wool circles, following the interfacing manufacturer's instructions.

2. Trim any interfacing that shows on the outside edge of the felted wool circles.

Sewing the Rows

1. Stitch the columns together 2 at a time so that it is easier to stitch the circles onto the openings.

2. Lay the wool circles over the openings in the hexagons.

3. Use a blanket stitch or your favorite method of appliqué to apply the circles to each pair of columns.

4. Stitch all the columns of the quilt together.

5. Appliqué circles to the remaining openings between the columns.

Finishing the Quilt

1. Layer, quilt, and bind the quilt using your favorite method.

2. To bind the peaked edges of the quilt, stitch the tops of the peaks as you would for the corners of a square quilt binding. To stitch the valleys, straighten the edge of the quilt. Arrange the extra bulk so that it is not under the needle and stitch across the valley.

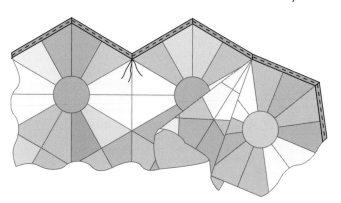